Malachi
God's Unchanging Love

Malachi
God's Unchanging Love

Walter C. Kaiser, Jr.

Baker Book House

Grand Rapids, Michigan 49506

Copyright 1984 by
Baker Book House Company

ISBN: 0-8010-5464-8

Second printing, June 1986

Scripture references are from the Revised Standard Version © 1962 by A. J. Holman
Company and from the New International Version © 1978 by New York International
Bible Society.

Printed in the United States of America

To The Evangelical Free Church
on the occasion of
One hundred years of ministry
in America
June, 1984
with
Thanks to God for
all that He has done through our churches
and with
Thanks to the E.F.C.A. for
their "love gift" of Trinity Evangelical Divinity School
to the body of Christ

Contents

Appendixes

Preface

If we are ever to bridge the gap between the "then" of the B.C. message of the Bible and the "now" of the contemporary audience of readers and listeners of the Word of God, we are going to need a whole new genus of commentary writing. It will need to contain some of the technical references traditionally found in exegetical commentaries along with legitimate application and exposition of that text to contemporary men and women such as one finds in printed sermons or homiletical notes on Biblical texts.

Now whether we name such a new genus a "homentary" (homiletics and commentary) or a "commelletics" is beside the point. The point is that exegesis has not finished its task when it has told us what the text meant to the writer of many centuries past; it must continue to work to the point of saying how those exegetically derived *meanings* yield legitimate *principles* that can be *applied* to contemporary listeners in a summons for action or response.

The work must also be simultaneously appropriate for use by the layreader as well as for the pastor/scholar. It must serve the spiritual as well as the technical needs of the *one* body of Christ. Therefore, toward that goal we offer this prototype of what we trust will be a whole new breed of commentary writing.

This work will simultaneously serve as a model to demonstrate the principles and argument we set forth earlier in *Toward an Exegetical Theology*. We have followed the procedures outlined there in part 2 of this present work, along with extensive side-by-side English and Hebrew block diagrams of the syntactical relationships found in the Book of Malachi. The outline suggested is intended to serve as a guide for any who wish to apply the same techniques to other passages of Scripture. It is our sincere hope and prayer that such procedures will lead to increased accuracy and depth of spiritual understanding in Bible studies, Sunday school lessons, para-church talks, and sermons.

It only remains for me to add how much I remain in the debt of others in the completing of this manuscript. I am deeply grateful to so many of God's people who first heard these messages on Malachi and added their comments and words of encouragement. Among the other friends who have also contributed an enormous amount of time and energy in bringing this work to the light of day are: my teaching assistant, Raymond Lubeck who helped compile the syntactical analysis and indices; Lois Armstrong, my administrative assistant and secretary who typed the entire manuscript in the midst of a very busy schedule; and the encouraging assistance given by project editor, Allan Fisher, and editor, Dan Van't Kerkhoff, of the Baker Book House.

Introduction

When times are hard, it is difficult to believe that God loves us. All appearances seem to count against such a belief. Yet, that is exactly what this little Book of Malachi is all about. Yahweh still loves Israel in spite of all appearances to the contrary. And this same unchanging Lord still loves us.

The Theme of Malachi

Naturally Malachi's audience found this bit of assurance most unnerving. The harshness of the times had so hardened them that they had veered toward a practical atheism with heavy dashes of hedonism and epicureanism. Therefore, they greeted Malachi's proclamation of the love of God with the scoffing skepticism of a Sadducee. Said they with biting sarcasm, "If God loves us, why doesn't he show it more? If he is so good and righteous, why aren't we seeing more evidence of prosperity and the fabulous days of the messianic era predicted by all the prophets?"

In their minds, the script for the postexilic era was much different from what they were experiencing. According to their understanding of the earlier prophets the land would rebound with miraculous fruitfulness (Ezek. 34:26–30), the population would swell to a mighty throng (Isa. 54:1–3), the nation would rise in esteem to the glorious reign of a new David (Jer. 23:5–6), and all nations would come and serve them (Isa. 49:22–23). But none of this was happening. The realities of the life were just the opposite. The land languished frequently under drought (Mal. 3:10), the population remained a fraction of what it had been, and the nation continued under the thumb of Persia and its governor (1:8).

But Malachi still maintained that God continued to love them. He also had a three-fold rebuttal for the heart of their complaint.

First of all, the harshness of their present lot in life was more than justified by the people's frigid formalism and outright disloyalty to their Lord—from the top (the priesthood) to the bottom of society (1:6–2:16; 2:17; 3:7–12). In brief, their suffering must be directly linked to their sins. Even the obvious failure of the people when it came to the ritual and cultic practices (1:8,14; 3:8) were in themselves only symptoms of a deeper sickness of the heart. Likewise, the sins against social morality (3:5) were only external evidences that there was no internal reality or fear of God.

Malachi's second answer to the people was that there were obvious evidences of God's love for Israel if only they would stop feeling sorry for themselves long enough to look around and note what was happening to their blood brothers the Edomites. Surely the grace of God had waited patiently since the days of 1800 to 1900 B.C., and now in the 500 to 400s B.C. the Nabatean Arabs were the instrument of God to visit final destruction on this nation (1:2–5). There was a law of righteousness and morality that operated inexorably in history (Jer. 18:7–9), for on more than one occasion the Edomites had either stood by refusing help or had urged the enemy on and joined in looting Israel when she was under attack (Ps. 137:7; Obad. 10–14; Amos 1:11–12; Jer. 49:7–22). Of course Israel too would have been subjected to removal from the historical scene had not God placed his unmerited election-love on her (Mal. 1:2, 3:6). It was because God did not change that the descendants of Jacob were not destroyed (3:6). And if she wished to know what she deserved, then she had only to look around her to nations like Edom to see what was happening. Just because God was long-suffering and patient with Persia was no reason to doubt that he was not also just and impartial in all his deeds and thought.

The third response of Malachi's is that a day of Yahweh is coming. In that day, final accounts with accompanying rewards and punishments would be rendered (3:16–4:6). This whole present order would be placed under God's judgment, and a whole new order would replace it with justice, righteousness, and the reign of the King himself. This eschatological view provided God's final answer to all who pressed for a solution to the problem of evil and suffering.

Naturally we cannot help observing that often, as was true of those who raised the objection in this book, such deep philosophical and theological questions are only ruses intended to divert one's own mind and the mind of others away from the real problem. Instead of being willing to penetrate to the heart of the matter and let the scalpel of God's Word cut out the cancerous growth found in the inner man, they preferred to play games and raise ponderous questions which were secondary outgrowths and only symptoms of their heart needs. Nevertheless, God did assure them—as he assures us still today—that a purpose runs through all history, and that purpose will be realized when this age has been overlapped and outstripped by the age to come in the last days.

This, then, is the central affirmation and the key argument of the book: God has, and continues, to love us, and no amount of doubting, objecting, or arguing the contrary will remove this fact.

The Author of Malachi

The prophet Malachi was the last of the series of Old Testament prophets. His name can be translated, "my messenger" or "my angel," but this may be an apocopated form for Malachiah ("Messenger of Yahweh" [see 2:7] or "Yahweh is my messenger") just as Abi ("my father") in 2 Kings 18:2 appears as Abijah ("Yahweh is my father") in 2 Chronicles 29:1.

The Septuagint and most modern commentators do not subscribe to the fact that Malachi is the personal name for the writer of this book, but they take it to be an official name or an appellative, i.e., "by the hand of *his* angel," (italics mine) a title borrowed for convenience sake from Malachi 3:1. But this view must change the pronoun "my" to a third person pronoun "his," for which there is no evidence. This fact only reinforces the originality and superiority of the Hebrew text and the personal name view advocated here.[1]

---

1. Joyce Baldwin, *Haggai, Zechariah, Malachi* (Downers Grove, Ill.: Inter-Varsity Press, 1972), p. 212.

There are, of course, many examples of apocopated names ending in -*î* in the Old Testament. For example, there is *Abi*, "my father," (2 Kings 18:2); Beeri, "my well" (Gen. 26:34; Hosea 1:1); Ethni, "my gift," (1 Chron. 6:41); Uri, "my fire, fiery," or perhaps "my light," (Exod. 31:2; 1 Kings 4:19; Ezra 10:24); and Zichri, "my remembrance(?)" (Exod. 6:21; 1 Chron. 8:19, 23, 27, etc.). So this may hardly be used against *mal'ākî* being a personal name.

There are other arguments that are supposed to count against Malachi's being a name: (1) the absence of any reference to his father (but the same is true of Obadiah); (2) the absence of the place of his birth (this is true also of several other prophets, e.g., Habakkuk); and (3) the fact that the last three "burdens" in the prophets (Zech. 9:1; 12:1; Mal. 1:1) share this same heading which probably marks all three as being anonymous additions to the collection of what is commonly called "the twelve [minor] prophets" (but if Zech. 9:1–14:21 is an integral part of his book, as many have pointed out on stylistic and linguistic grounds, then this argument also falls).

In the Jewish tradition, the person of Malachi was remembered along with Haggai and Zechariah as men of the great synagogue. The Targum of Jonathan,[2] Jerome, and the Rabbi Rashi (1040–1105) understood Malachi as a title for Ezra the Scribe; a view which Calvin preferred.[3] Pseudo Epiphanius and other church fathers[4] linked Malachi with a town of Sopha or Sophira in Zubulun[5] and called him a Levite.

Since there are no valid reasons that can be brought against the argument that this is a real name, we prefer to argue that, in accordance with the practice of all the preceding writing prophets, Malachi also is not an anonymous work, but is written by a

2. After the word "Malachi," this targum adds, "who otherwise is called the scribe Ezra." Note Hag. 1:13; Haggai is called "the messenger of Yahweh."

3. John Calvin, *The Twelve Minor Prophets* (Edinburgh: T & T Clark, 1849), V: 459.

4. Cf. statements by Dorotheus, Ephraem Syrus, Hesychius, and Isidorus Hisp, as cited by John M. P. Smith, *Book of Malachi,* International Critical Commentary, (Edinburgh: T & T Clark, 1912), p. 10.

5. *Epiphanius, Vitae prophetarum* as cited by John M. P. Smith, ibid, from Nestle's *Marginalien,* p. 28 f.

prophet named Malachi who *may* have been a priest and *may* have come from Sopha of Zebulun.

The Date of Malachi

There is fairly widespread agreement on the general area in which we are to date this prophecy. All agree that it must come after the days in which Haggai and Zechariah prophesied beginning in 520 B.C., since Malachi 1:6–14, and 3:10 assume that the temple worship has been restored in this postexilic age. And since Ben Sira (-Ecclesiasticus) 48:10[6] quotes Malachi 4:6, a date in the Maccabean era for Malachi is totally out of the question. Indeed, Ecclesiasticus 49:10 demonstrates that in approximately 180 B.C. the book of the twelve prophets was already recognized as canonical and included the prophecy of Malachi.

The only historical reference in Malachi is the destruction of Edom[7] (1:3–5). This destruction may be the one carried out under Nebuchadnezzar in his 587 B.C. campaigns on Jerusalem and the surrounding nations or, more likely, the one effected by the Nabatean Arabs[8] who totally drove out the Edomites between 550 and 400 B.C., setting up their own Idumean state in its place. Unfortunately we cannot date this latter event with any degree of precision. Therefore we must rely on other internal clues from the book.

The strongest clues are to be found in the agreements that exist between Malachi and Nehemiah. Furthermore, since Malachi predicates several of his arguments on the existence and the knowledge of the law of Moses (e.g., 4:4), the book must be dated after the time of Ezra's arrival in Judah in 458 B.C., for it was Ezra who restored the knowledge and authority of the law of God (Ezra 7:14, 25, 26). Moreover, prior to Ezra's arrival, the costs of worship-

---

6. "O Elias [the prophet] . . . who was ordained for reproofs in their times to pacify the wrath of God's judgment . . . and *to turn the heart of the father unto the son,* and to restore the tribes of Jacob" (italics mine).

7. J.R. Bartlett, "The Moabites and Edomites," in *Peoples of Old Testament Times,* ed. D. J. Wiseman (Oxford: Clarendon, 1973), pp. 229–58.

8. John Irving Lawlor, *The Nabataeans in Historical Perspective* (Grand Rapids: Baker, 1974); and Philip C. Hammond, "New Light on the Nabataeans," *Biblical Archaeology Review* 7(1981): 22–43.

ing God were paid out of the royal revenues of Persia (7:15–17, 20–24). It was only afterward (6:9–10) that the abuses found in Malachi 1:6–9 could have sprung up.

The term "governor" in Malachi 1:8 may imply the interval of time between Ezra's arrival in 458 B.C. and the coming of Nehemiah in 445 B.C. Nehemiah 5:14 makes it clear that there were other governors prior to Nehemiah, and the Elephantine papyri also show that there were other governors beside Zerubbabel and Nehemiah. No doubt the Persians took over the term "governor" (*peḥah*), which was used under the Babylonian domination (Jer. 51:28, 57; Ezek, 23:6) even though their normal title was *tiršātâh* (Neh. 10:1 [2]; but see Esther 3:12 and Neh. 5:14). Many believe that if Nehemiah had been this governor, Malachi would have named him just as Haggai named Zerubbabel. Thus, those who weigh this argument heavily place the book between 458 and 445 B.C. or in the indeterminate length of time between the end of Nehemiah's twelve years of governing in 433 B.C. and his return to govern again (Neh. 13:9–11, 19, 21). This would place Malachi's ministry after 433 B.C.[9]

But all agree that Malachi shared many of the same concerns that Nehemiah did.

1. Marriage of heathen wives
   (Mal. 2:11–15 and Neh. 13:23–27)
2. Neglect in paying the tithes
   (Mal. 3:8–10 and Neh. 13:10–14)
3. Disregard of the Sabbath
   (Mal. 2:8–9; 4:4 and Neh. 13:15–22)
4. Corruption of the priesthood
   (Mal. 1:6–2:9 and Neh. 13:7–9)
5. Existence of social wrongs
   (Mal. 3:5 and Neh. 5:1–13).

Thus the date for Malachi could fit into several slots very nicely: during Nehemiah's absence from Jerusalem, during Nehemiah's second visit and governorship, or after Nehemiah's second term

9. W.J. Dumbrell, "Malachi and the Ezra-Nehemiah Reforms," *The Reformed Theological Review* 35(1976): 42–52.

of office. On the whole it may be best to see Malachi as a kind of forerunner who prepared for the extensive reforms introduced by Nehemiah when he returned sometime after 433 B.C. This would also fit the extensive parallels to Nehemiah 13.

The Divisions of Malachi

Traditionally, commentators have divided this prophecy into six sections as follows:

1. **1:1–5** Introduction. God proves his love for Israel by contrasting it with the condition of Edom.
2. **1:6–2:9** Rebuke of the priesthood for their perversion of the ordinances and law of God.
3. **2:10–16** Rebuke for perverting God's ordinance of marriage by marrying unbelieving partners and divorcing previous wives.
4. **2:17–3:6** The announcement of God's messenger who will prepare the way for his Messiah as his answer to the search for the justice of God.
5. **3:7–12** Rebuke of the people for withholding the tithes and offerings owed to God.
6. **3:13–4:6** Prediction of the destiny of the wicked and the righteous.

While we acknowledge that these six sections make good sense, we will treat the section in five messages instead of six. There is complete agreement on the first (1:1–5) and sixth sections (3:13–4:6), but we have chosen to limit the second message to 1:6–14 for two reasons: (1) the section has a suitable climax in 1:14, and (2) there is already more material than can be easily handled in most messages.

Even though the rebuke for the priests continues into 2:1–9, the type of admonishment easily fits together with the style and types of concern in verses 10–16. Therefore, our third message will treat 2:1–16.

Finally, we have combined sections four and five since we see much integration here. Verse 6 applies as much to 3:1–5 as it does to verses 7–12. Hence, our fourth message will extend from the question raised in 2:17 to 3:12.

The Style of Malachi

Malachi is a gem in its clarity, simplicity, and directness. Out of its fifty-five verses, forty-seven are first-person addresses of the Lord to Israel.

It is customary for some to make various types of disparaging remarks about the literary skills of this Hebrew prophet as compared to an Isaiah or Amos. But all such opinions are just that, and the standard by which these evaluations are being made are seldom explicitly given.

Malachi composed his work in a prose rather than a poetic format. The most distinctive trait of his prose is the disputational method that he adopted to introduce many of his main sections. In fact, his message is constantly punctuated with questions from both his audience and his Lord (1:2,6,7,8,9,13; 2:10,14,15,17; 3:2,7,8,13).

Most typically Malachi will introduce a new declaration from God only to record the audience rebuttal with the introductory words, "you say" (1:2,6,7,13; 2:14,17; 3:7,8,13). Even though other prophets had engaged in exchanges with their audiences (e.g., Isa. 40:27,28; Jer. 2:23–25, 29–34, 35–36; 8:8–9; and Ezek. 12:21–28), Malachi is the master of this technique.[10] With adroitness and consummate skill, he fields each of the protestations offered by his audience. How pathetic are their questions! They reflect such artificial piety and such a gross misunderstanding of the program and message of God. Nevertheless, Malachi will not be sidetracked from his theme. God still loves them, and that love will pursue even the most hypocritical and insincere.[11]

One is struck with the majesty of God in this book. He, indeed, is Master, Lord, and King. The greatness of the name of God (1:5,11,14; 2:2) and the success of his coming Messiah and the day

---

10. James A. Fischer, "Notes on the Literary Form and Message of Malachi," *Catholic Biblical Quarterly* 34(1972): 315–20.

11. Roddy Braun, "Malachi—A Catechism for Times of Disappointment," *Currents in Theology and Mission* 4(1977): 297–303.

of the Lord stand sure in spite of the lack of respect from his people. But there is a believing remnant that still "fear[s] the Lord" (another theme frequently repeated. 1:6,11,14; 2:5; 3:5,16; 4:2,5). The two pivotal statements of the book are found in 1:2 and 3:6: "I have loved you" and "I the Lord change not." Therefore, *Malachi: God's Unchanging Love* seems a fitting title for this book.

1

A Call to Respond to God's Love

(Malachi 1:1–5)

The theme of Malachi's first message is the theme of the whole book, "I have loved you, says the Lord" (1:2). Like a banner over a Bible conference, this theme of the love of God must stand as the masthead over every page. His banner over us is love!

God's love goes beyond all attempts to explain its causes or all tests of its durability. Yet it also was the foundation on which each of his complaints against Israel was lodged. In view of all the mercies and persistent love of God, how could his people exhibit such ingratitude, hypocrisy, and mistaken notions about his love?

The Hebrew verb "to love" ('āhab) is used thirty-two times of God's love in the Old Testament, twenty-three of which are cases of his loving Israel or particular individuals. The noun form occurs four times for God's love of his people, giving us a total of twenty-seven times God's love for man is affirmed.[1]

Snaith lays down three main characteristics that help us understand God's love. First, that love is a sovereign love. The fact that God is King and in control of all is deeply embedded in the Biblical materials. As Lord over all, no necessity is laid

---

1. Norman H. Snaith, *Distinctive Ideas of the Old Testament* (London: Epworth Press, 1944), p. 132. "On the other hand, the verb is used twenty-two times of man's love for God; nineteen of man loving God's Name, Law, precepts, etc., and twice of man loving Jerusalem."

21

on him. The norm is marked out by his own character and being. Accordingly there is no definition of love apart from what he is and how he acts, just as there is no understanding of what justice is apart from him, for both love and justice are derived from him.

The second characteristic of God's love is that it is unconditional. "The LORD did not set his love upon [us], nor choose [us], because [we] were more in number than any people; for [we; and especially Israel] were the fewest of all people: But because the LORD loved [us], and because he would keep the oath which he had sworn unto [our] fathers " (Deut. 7:7–8). Over and over again we find that the motivating reason or cause of his love for his people lay entirely on God's side, or as the text says so frequently for his own sake or for his name's sake (2 Kings 19:34; 20:6; Pss. 22:3; 25:11(12); 31:3(4); 79:9; 106:8; 109:21; 143:11; Isa. 37:35; 43:25; 48:11; Jer. 14:7,21; Ezek. 20:9,22,44). This expression simply meant that Jehovah loved his people because that is what he is like. He loved them and he loves us for no other reason outside himself than that he would love them and us. Story after story stresses the true, but often unpleasant fact, that there was not the least degree of good, beauty, or desirability in the people who were the objects of his love. Whether it be the unpleasant details of Ezekiel 16:4–6 or those of Hosea 11:1–3, the conclusion was always the same: God's love for his people was unconditioned. In fact, when God found Israel she was in a state that ordinarily would have brought forth the reactions of revulsion rather than love. We cannot even say that God loved Israel because he saw possibilities that no one else saw. This is inadequate because it would be true of anyone the Lord might choose—anyone would have boundless possibilities. God loves where there is nothing to love, nothing worthy of love, and his is a wholly disinterested love. He loved simply because he *would* love. He is love!

The third characteristic of God's love is that it is intimately personal. Moses finds it amazing that the God to whom "belong the heaven and the heaven of heavens, the earth with all that is in it" should *in the face of all this* (the Hebrew restrictive adverb *raq*, "only" or "yet" in v. 15) set his affection personally on Israel and their descendants (Deut. 10:14–15). So personal was that love that Hosea could depict it as a father taking his son by the arms while he still was an infant and teaching him how to walk (Hos. 11:1–3). God would draw his people with cords, but not ordinary ropes; these were the cords of love (11:4). His love was an intimately personal love.

But one more characteristic must be added to this. God's love can best be compared to the love that exists between a husband and a wife. In other analogies we have lesser glimpses of what God's love for us is like. In C. S. Lewis' four analogies of love there is: (1) the love of the artist for the artifact he or she has created, (2) the love a master has for a dog or pet, (3) the love of parents for their child, and (4) the love between a husband and a wife.[2] But it is the fourth that helps us to define God's love in the most unique way. His love, like that which exists between a husband and a wife, is willing to forgive the most (because love is willing to look beyond, and to pay the price for, the worst of faults), yet is a love that condones the least (because that love, while continuing to forgive, never ceases coaxing, urging, wishing, and hoping for the best in the other partner). In the same way God's way is the most generous in offering us pardon and acceptance while it still maintains the high and holy standard of his righteousness to which he calls us. Rather than giving up on and tending to condone our sins and failures to meet his high standards, he faithfully continues to love us without making excuses for our failures or deciding that he must lower the standard to meet us where we are. It is precisely in this tension of forgiving the most and condoning the least that we can understand the uniqueness of God's love. It is this characteristic that explains how he can call for justice to be meted out in judgment, protesting at the same time, "I have loved you."

This raises the whole question of how to reconcile the anger of God (ira dei) with the love of God. In the history of the church, this became the question of divine passibility (i.e., whether God was capable of having feelings or emotions); or was God impassible (i.e., without a capacity to feel, suffer, or be angry)?

Gnosticism took a strong lead in the discussion by denying that God could ever experience anger, feelings, or suffer at all. And a second-century heretic named Marcion declared that God was

---

2. C. S. Lewis, *The Problem of Pain*, (New York: Macmillan Co., 1953), pp. 30–6.

totally free of all affections or feelings, and was incapable of getting angry—Marcion's god was totally apathetic.

It was the church father, Lactantius, (last half of the third century) who put the question in a more Biblical perspective. Lactantius argued this way: "He who loves the good also hates the evil, and he who does not hate the evil does not love the good because, on the one hand, to love the good comes from hatred of evil and to hate the evil rises from the love of the good."[3]

Our problem with anger in the character of God is usually the result of our poor definitions. Anger is not what Aristotle argued, "the desire for retaliation" or a desire to get even for some slight or actual harm done.[4] Anger, as rightly defined by Lactantius, is "a motion of the soul rousing itself to curb sin."[5] But anger must not be left unchecked or uncontrolled. God's anger is never explosive, unexplainable, or unreasonable. It never controls him, nor does it shut off his mercies and compassions from us (Ps. 77:9). Instead it marks the end of his indifference: he cannot and will not remain neutral in the face of our sin. But in comparison to his love, his anger passes quickly (Isa. 26:20; 54:7–8; 57:16–19) while his love remains (Jer. 31:3; Hos. 2:19). This, then, is the type of divine love that Malachi portrays.

The announcement of this love occupies Malachi's first message. Since God's love had continued unabated, there was a call for Israel to reciprocate in kind. Indeed, there were three *evidences* (our homiletical keyword) of God's love, and these were sufficient in themselves to constitute a basis for a new summons to Israel that she love God as he had loved her. The evidences were these:

> Our God's election-love—1:1–3
>
> Our God's justice-love—1:4
>
> Our God's universal-love—1:5

Let us look at each of these three evidences in turn.

3. Lactantius, *The Minor Works: De Ira Dei* [The Wrath of God], trans. Sister Mary Francis McDonald (Washington DC: Catholic University of America Press, 1965), Vol. 154:69.

4. Aristotle, *De Anima*, I,1. Also cited by Lactantius, *The Minor Works*, p. 101.

5. As cited by Abraham Heschel, *The Prophets*, 2 vols. (New York: Harper & Row, 1962), II, 82.

Our God's Election-Love (1:1–3)

The message of God's love for his people is introduced as a "burden" (*maśśā'*). While most modern commentators insist on translating this word as "oracle" or a "declaration," many in-depth studies agree in seeing some ominous aspect to its meaning.

E. W. Hengstenberg[6] gave these reasons for finding that *maśśā'* was a prophetic speech of a threatening or minatory character:

1. The word appears twenty-seven times, all in prophetic contexts of threatened judgment with the exception of Proverbs 30:1; 31:1.
2. The word is never followed by the genitive of speaker such as *ne'um* of Yahweh, but it is always connected with a genitive of an object (such as the *maśśā'* of Babylon, of Moab, etc.) unless an additional item such as "the word of the LORD" (cf. Mal. 1:1; 3:1; Zech. 9:1) intervenes.[7]
3. There are no examples of a noun derived from a hypothetical root *nāśā'* with the sense of "to utter" that would yield the meaning "oracle," "declaration," or the like.

In a more recent study, P. A. H. de Boer concluded that he failed to find any evidence in the Hebrew lexicography for two words behind *maśśā'*, one meaning "load" and the other "oracle." He concluded that there was a single meaning for all the occurrences. *Maśśā'* was a burden "imposed by a master, a despot or a deity on their subjects, men or things."[8]

Thus our prophecy opens on a threatening note even though it will simultaneously exalt God's love for his people. As in Zechariah 9:1 and 12:1, so here in Malachi 1:1 there is the conviction that

6. E. W. Hengstenberg, *Christology of the Old Testament*, 4 vols. tr. James Martin (Edinburgh: T & T Clark, 1875), III: 339–43. See also Walter C. Kaiser, Jr., *"maśśā',"* *Theological Wordbook of the Old Testament* (TWOT), 2 vols. (Chicago: Moody Press, 1980), II, 602.

7. P. A. H. de Boer, "An Inquiry into the Meaning of the Term *Massā"* as cited by Baldwin, *Haggai, Zechariah, Malachi*, pp. 162–63.

8. de Boer, p. 214.

God is going to come soon to judge the world. The heavy note of this message was to stir up men and women to prepare for that day. Like a cloud, God's judgment hung over the people if they did not repent.

God's ominous note of judgment was to be found in his "word" (the same connection of "burden" and "word" is made in Zech. 9:1 and 12:1). It was a word directed to "Israel," a name which on previous occasions had signified only the northern ten tribes, but which now represented the whole Jewish community, even as the name had always continued to mean even during the period of the specialized use.

God's word came by the hand of or through the agency of his prophet Malachi. While the same Hebrew word appears in Malachi 3:1, there it is translated "my messenger." But here, contrary to the Septuagint and the Targumim, it probably is a proper name and not a common noun (see Introduction).

Abruptly Malachi breaks into his message and the theme of his first message: "I have loved you." The tense of the verb (Hebrew, perfect tense) makes it clear that God's love has not only operated in the past, but it also is presently in effect as well. The idea was not a novel one, for repeatedly God had announced his love as his only cause for choosing Israel (Deut. 7:7; 10:18, Hos. 11:1, etc.). But it was necessary to raise the sights of a people who had become skeptical as to whether that love was still in effect.

Such a generous announcement only brought the most incredible response from the people: In what has he loved us? (Mal. 1:2). And there the heart of the matter lay bare. They were insensitive to both the love of God and to their own wicked departure from God.

That God would even condescend to answer such brashness is a further illustration of his patient love, but he did offer to give an illustration of that love. It was to be found in his election-love of Jacob vis-á-vis his "hatred" (śānē') of Esau.[9]

Does this then imply that Yahweh is hateful? It is true that there are clear objects that merit God's hate (e.g., hypocritical worship in Isa. 1:14 and Amos 5:21; or the seven evils of Prov. 6:16–19

9. See J. A. Thompson, "Israel's 'Haters,'" *Vetus Testamentum* 29(1979): 200-205. The terms "love" and "hate" are used in the religious realm for those who acknowledge Yahweh's lordship and those who do not.

including pride, lying, murder, evil imagination, evil-doing, false witness, and dissension among the brethren), and that even the sinless incarnate Son of God was, on occasion, filled with emotions of anger (e.g., at the grave of Lazarus, John 11:33,38; also Mark 3:5, 10:14; and John 2:17). Hate can be a proper emotion for disavowing, differentiating, and espousing its opposite—love. Only one who has truly loved can understand how it is possible to hate with a burning anger all that is wrong and evil.

But there is also a specialized use of the antonymic pair, "to love" and "to hate." A close parallel to the Jacob and Esau situation can be seen in the case of Rachel and Leah in Genesis 29:30–33 or the case of the two wives who were not equally loved in Deuteronomy 21:15–17. To put the matter bluntly, the "hated" wife in both these relationships was the *less-loved* one. This same nuance of meaning has carried over in the Semitism found in the Greek antonyomic use of *agapan/misein* in Matthew 6:24 and Luke 16:13. "To love" is, in effect, *to prefer* or be faithful to one while "to hate" is to slight or *think less of* another. In two parallel lists in the New Testament, Matthew 10:37 uses the formula *ho philōn huper eme*, "He who loves . . . more than me," while Luke 14:26 parallels it by saying "if anyone comes to me [*kai ou misei*] and does not hate . . ."

Thus the reference to Esau, (just as the New Testament allusion of Jesus to fathers, mothers, wives, children, brothers, and sisters) does not call for a psychological or absolute hatred, but a ranking, a preference, a setting of priorities for higher purposes and goals that demand concentrated effort. In Jacob's case, God's love signaled his election and his call for service (i.e., to be a blessing to all the nations on the earth—including Esau's nation of Edom). Esau was not, therefore, the object of God's disdain, disgust, and unchecked design for revenge, for he too was the object of God's preached word (note the addressees in Obadiah) and the objects of his deliverance in the end times (cf. Obad. 19, 21; Amos 9:12).

God's "love" and "hate" (in this sense of choosing as the object of his purposeful-love and deciding not to prefer for a certain task) was made apart from anything these men were or did. God's choice of Jacob, for example, took place *before* Jacob was born (Gen. 25:23; cf. Rom. 9:11). Thus once again we are brought face to face with the sovereign, unconditional, intimately personal, and discriminating love of God (see general introduction for a definition of these four characteristics of God's love).

Our God's Justice-Love (1:3b–4)

But there is more here than just the electing love of God. True, God's election-love had sustained a wicked Israel that more than deserved to be reduced to rubble (Mal. 3:6 had said the same: "I the LORD do not change; therefore you, O sons of Jacob, are not consumed"). But with the absence of that sustaining love, Edom's (Jacob's brother—nation) mountains had been turned into a wasteland, and his inheritance had been left to the desert jackals (1:3b).

We are not sure when this destruction of Edom took place. It was either the one Nebuchadnezzar introduced when he also leveled Judah in 587 B.C. (Jer. 49:7–9; 25:9, 21) or, more likely, the one accomplished by Nabatean Arabs somewhere around 550 to 400 B.C. The Nabateans ransacked Edom leaving only pockets of Edomite refugees in the Negev desert (I Macc. 5:25). It was these same Nabateans who set up the country of Idumea (4:29; Mark 3:8) with its capital in Hebron and one of its great cities, built into the cliffs, named Petra.

Esau, of course, could hardly be surprised at such an outcome, for he had become "immoral" and "godless" as both the Old Testament and New Testament testify (cf. Gen. 25:32; 36:1–8; Heb. 12:16). Thus, while God's election-love called one man to his service, both were required to walk in the light of his word; for only in the obedience of faith could either Jacob or Esau participate in the promise of God—even though Jacob must *transmit* the blessing to later generations of his descendants whether he personally *participated* in them or not.

God's love will condone the least when it witnesses sin in the life. The same love that calls men to himself must also discriminate against evil. The judgment of God against Esau/Edom must now also serve to warn skeptical Jacob and the present day Christian church.

In verse 4, Edom exudes confidence in his own ability to restore everything as it had been prior to the devastating blow of the enemy. However, without God's help (as was true in Jacob's situation in spite of the disbelief of the populace), the exercise was doomed to failure. All such privileges and accomplishments come from the hand of God. Edom might build again, but "the Lord of hosts"[10] would tear it down (a group of verbs reminiscent of the key verbs in Jeremiah's call) (1:10; cf. also 5:17 and 9:11).

Instead Edom would be known as "the wicked country" (Mal. 1:4b). Sin had left its mark on both the people and the land. Whereas the anger of God was felt on Jerusalem for her sin, that was but a brief problem compared to Edom's embarrassment, which would be perpetual. The quiet ruin of Petra stands as a mute testimony to the truthfulness of God's word.

God's Universal-Love (1:5)

Even though Israel was most insensitive to the love and favor of God, there will come a time when she will be forced to acknowledge the unmerited favor of God. Had the people looked beyond the provincialism of their own distress, Israel could have clearly seen the contrast between what had happened to Edom, now these decades later, and what had taken place in the case of Israel. There were worlds of difference, but Israel's own internal difficulties had kept her from taking the wider look of God's dealings with all nations.

But what is that the people would say? Would they say, "The Lord will be magnified *beyond* (*mē'al*) the border of Israel?" or "The Lord will be magnified *above* the border of Israel?" Both renderings are possible, but which one did Malachi mean? Since verses 11 and 14 praise God as a great king over all nations, it would appear that the first rendering is to be preferred—"beyond."

God's love, in its graciousness and in its judgments, exceeded traditional national, political, geographic, or cultural boundaries. It would *go beyond* them, even as God had promised Abraham

10. "The Lord of hosts" probably conveys the idea of "he who is sovereign over the 'hosts' (armies) of heaven and earth." The Septuagint translates it *pantokratōn*, "almighty" twenty-four times in Malachi. This translation passes over into the New Testament in 1 Cor. 6:18, "The Lord Almighty," "The Almighty" in Rev. 1:8, or "The Lord God Almighty" in Rev. 4:8 and elsewhere.

when he first called him and set his love on him in Genesis 12:1–3: "In your seed, all the nations of the earth shall be blessed." This "blessing" Paul easily labeled as the "good news," or "gospel," in Galatians 3:8.

How we should praise God that his love was meant to be universal and extend beyond the borders of Israel. It can also be observed that since the future verb precedes the subject, it may be best to translate the verb in verse 5b as an optative rather than as a future:[11] "May Yahweh be magnified (or 'exalted, praised') beyond the borders of Israel"[12] as it is in Psalm 35:27 or in 40:16 (17).

Just as God had brought judgment on Pharaoh and the Egyptians so that they and all the world might know that the Lord is God, so he had done the same to Edom. They, and we, can only acknowledge that his name is to be praised in the face of all his marvelous works. His love indeed is amazing.

We conclude that there is much evidence for the love of God. That love set forth the offer of salvation we have inherited from Jacob. It is also the love that has reached out in its justice and in its nonparochial graciousness to deal with evil and to offer salvation to all mankind.

But we must be careful not to doubt that love just because we may be in some affliction, like the struggling remnant of Malachi's day. When God says that he has loved us in the past and has continued to love us in the present, we must believe him instead of insultingly demanding, "Where is the proof?"

The threatenings of God are heavy and they do constitute a burden for all who will not receive his freely proffered love. But the glory of God will far exceed all the terrors and ambitions of man. May God be praised beyond the borders of Israel in every land and by every tongue, tribe and nation. His love, indeed, is inscrutably great and past finding out.

11. Joseph Packard, *The Book of Malachi Expounded,* Lange's Commentary (New York: Scribner, Armstrong. . . . , 1876), p. 8.

12. This prepositional phrase is also found in Gen. 1:7; 1 Sam. 17:39; Ezek. 1:25; Neh. 12:31, 37, 39; 2 Chron. 13:4; 24:20; 26:19; Jon. 4:6 according to John Merlin Powis Smith, *A Critical and Exegetical Commentary on the Book of Malachi,* The International Critical Commentary (ICC), (Edinburgh: T & T Clark, 1912), p. 23. He found that it always meant "over," "above" or "upon," but not "beyond" even though he cited sixteen commentators who preferred the meaning "beyond" for this context!

2

A Call to Be Authentic
(Malachi 1:6–14)

Not too many years ago the fashion was to charge the older generation, institutions, administrators, big business, and the government with being false, insincere, and generally untrustworthy. Those who told things as they really were, viz., the collegiate generation of the sixties and early seventies, were the only authentic and credible people! At least, that is what they said.

We may be able to smile at such superciliousness now that we are safely beyond the seriousness of those days, but this will not excuse us for not heeding the divine call to an authenticity that exceeds all current fashions, slogans, or eddies of our day. There is indeed a credibility gap, but it is not located primarily in the news releases of our governments or in the mass media or the advertisements of big businesses. To be sure, these all have their problems; but even more basic is the issue of the credibility and the authenticity gap of the clergy, for as go the clergy so goes a people.

Malachi took dead aim on the priests of his day (1:6) and delivered a stinging indictment on their careless, haphazard, and profane service to the living God. But lest it be thought that the only possible relevance this text has is for contemporary clergy, we assure the reader that Malachi 1:14 immediately enlarges its intended audience to all believers. "Cursed is the cheat who has a male in his flock, and vows it, and yet sacrifices to the Lord what is blemished." Suddenly, in a context primarily addressed to priests or the clergy, the focus is extended to include any and all Israelites who are indulging in the same type of practices. It would appear perfectly proper, then, to assume that what has been addressed to the priests is equally true for the laity as well.

The connection of this section with the preceding (Mal. 1:1–5 in our chap. 1) is fairly transparent. The banner, as it were, over those opening five verses was " 'I have loved you,' says the Lord." Since there was no reason for persisting in their doubts about the fact that God had always loved his people and that he continued to do so, the prophet then moved to point out why that divine love was unable to demonstrate itself fully. It was sheer indifference, carelessness, and half-heartedness, primarily on the part of the spiritual leadership, and then among the people at large, that blocked the full effects of the people's privileged position and election from showing through in God's love. The result was a heap of curses rather than blessings (vv. 11–14).

Once again, the special conversational style of this book breaks through with a repeated protest of innocence in the question, "Who? Us? We did that? We are guilty of that?" That feigned naiveté had already been used in Malachi 1:2 as the people's response to God's announcement of his love for them. They coolly retorted, "In what way did you love us?" "We seem to have missed it"—or words to that effect. Now in 1:6–14, they use this same artifice twice, in verse 6 and again in verse 7. All together, Malachi's audience will do so seven times in the scope of this brief book.

The analysis of the paragraphing, or subunits, within the larger unit for these nine verses may be arranged in this manner:

vv. 6–7   an introductory divine proverb
                  a question based on the proverb
                  an innocent protestation as a response
                  a divine answer

vv. 8–9   a probing question from God
                  an ironical suggestion

> a follow-up question
> an exposé and reason for clerical ineffectiveness

vv. 10–12   a divine challenge
> a divine estimation of worship
> [an evangelical interruption—v. 11]
> a divine rebuke

vv. 13–14   a report of a popular conclusion
> a report of the sad state of affairs
> a divine question filled with reproof
> a declaration of greatness

We conclude then the text has four separate movements or separate thoughts that develop the overall theme of a call to be authentic. They appear to address four *areas* (our homiletic keyword) and direct the believer's attention to authentic and credible living in these four areas:

> Our profession—1:6–7
>
> Our gifts—1:8–9
>
> Our service—1:10–12
>
> Our time—1:13–14

The focus of the section is not on man, for that very quickly could evaporate into a mere paralysis of analysis and measuring of reality by man. But the pattern and full measure to which we and Malachi's audience are being called can be seen in the *focal point* of the section, which is repeated three times: twice in verse 11, "my name is [(or) will be] great among the nations"; and in verse 14, "my name is [(or) will be] feared among the nations." To this is added, as it were, the signature of our God, "for I am a great King" (v. 14).

That is the model of excellence, reality, and authenticity to which men and women are being challenged. In direct proportion to which mortals grasp the greatness of the person, character, and attributes of God (-his name), to that degree will their own inadequacies, falseness, and diluted worship take on credibility, substance, acceptance, and posture. Let us take up Malachi's call then, to be authentic.

In Our Profession (1:6–7)

God had chosen Jacob as his "son" (Exod. 4:22; Hos. 11:1; Jer. 31:9)[1] and his "servant"[2] (especially in the role "Servant of the Lord," Isa. 41:8 and nineteen more times between Isa. 41:8 and 53:11). This adoption and election had a double edge to it, for it was an election for service as well as for privilege. The scope of each term, "son" and "servant," took on such technical status that it moved from the single individual Jacob to embrace all who likewise believed from among the Israelites and the nations. Yet it could also be so narrowed in perspective that it would yield up its final representative who at once was the epitome and the consummation of the whole group. That is why "my son" and "my servant" or the "servant of the Lord" can serve at one and the same time for all the believers in Israel and also be messianic.[3] The oscillation between the single and the plural, interestingly enough, was always thought of by the writers as part of their single truth-intention. It was as if they received a revelatory word which had an immediate historical fulfillment or several fulfillments, but which historical enactment in their immediate context operated as an earnest, harbinger, or downpayment on the final and ultimate event which the prophet could also see perfectly lined up with these fulfilled events in his own historical context. Together they formed one whole. Graphically it would appear as in figure 1.

Thus God's son was Jacob, then each one of the believing community—especially those in the Davidic line—and then that final Davidite, Christ! Accordingly, the prophets treated such terms, which acquired technical status, as having one sense or one meaning even though they experienced multiple fulfillments as God continued to maintain his prophetic word by working in the historical process.

But our usage of "son" and "servant" begins in a type of proverbial saying: Sons [generally] honor their father and ser-

1. Cf. Psa. 68:5; 89:26; 103:13; Isa. 9:6; 43:6; 63:16; 64:8.

2. The worshiper as God's "slave" or "servant" can be seen in Exod. 3:12; 9:1; 1 Sam. 3:9; 1 Kings 8:66; Ezra 5:11; Zech. 3:9.

3. Walter C. Kaiser, Jr., *Toward an Old Testament Theology* (Grand Rapids: Zondervan, 1978), pp. 101–13, 215–17.

Figure 1
Prophetic View

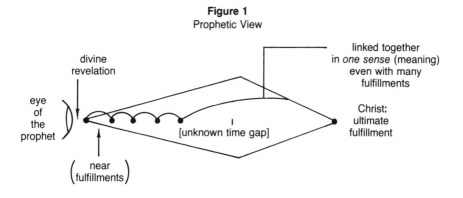

vants [generally] fear their master. That is as things should have been, but therein lay the irony as well. And Malachi took dead aim on the priests and pointedly asked, "If I am master or Lord [as you profess so loudly and publicly], where is my fear? If I am father [as you also seem to affirm], where is my honor?"

No doubt there was both a professed relationship (he is our Father and our Lord) and a profession of faith and creed (we honor our Father and we fear our Lord). But, both the relationship and the life belied the fact that something was desperately out of touch with reality here.

It was so unnatural and so embarrassing. How could a man's life be so completely separate from his words—all protestations to the contrary? Customarily (the proverb stresses this fact with its use of the "tense" for customary action) sons "honor" their father.

The term used for "fear" appears over one hundred times in the Biblical texts alongside of loving and serving God, e.g., "What does the LORD your God require of you, but to fear the LORD your God, to walk in all his ways, to love him, and to serve the LORD your God with all your heart and with all your soul" (Deut. 10:12). In fact, there are two kinds of fear in the Old Testament; both use the same word, but they are worlds apart in meaning. Both appear in a single verse in Exodus 20:20: "Do not fear; for God has come to prove you, and that the fear of him might be before your eyes, that you might not sin." Don't be frightened or scared, urged one use for "fear"; only "believe" or "trust" him urged the other use of the same word. Thus a whole soul attitude and response of trusting God as one's Lord and Master was wrapped up in this one positive use of the verb "to fear."

Such a refusal to dedicate to God real honor and trust, the kind that rightfully belonged to one's heavenly Father and the Master of the whole universe from all claiming to be true sons and daughters, was an outright despising of the majestic name of God.[4] His "name" was a disclosure of his very being and person (Exod. 23:20,21; Deut. 28:58), of his doctrine (Ps. 22:22; John 17:6, 26), of his authority (Matt. 7:22; Mark 9:39; Acts 4:7), and of his attributes. But when those charged with "true instruction," "guarding knowledge", and with being a source from whom "men should seek instruction" (2:6–7) failed to honor and fear that name and what it stood for, then they belittled God's greatness and majesty; they demeaned his reputation among Israel and the nations (compare vv. 11 and 14)!

However, never at a loss for words, these arrogant imposters of true religion rallied to turn the question back against God and his prophet. "How's that? When have we ever despised your name?" they replied in self-righteous indignity. One can almost see them standing there chorusing their answers almost as if they had rehearsed the whole thing ahead of time.

Every time I read Malachi I cannot help associating an experience I had many years ago now. My new bride and I had just moved into a rather large home in a college community as house parents for thirteen young freshman at the same Christian college where I had just begun as a freshman instructor in Bible. About two one morning, I was awakened by a tremendous clamor coming from the rooms upstairs. I was yanked from the clutches of sound sleep and as if by instinct and remembrance of a line from the poetry of Christmas, "I sprang to my feet to see what was the matter." Half asleep, but filled with resolve, I trudged out of

---

4. See Walter C. Kaiser, Jr., "Name" in *Zondervan Pictorial Encyclopedia of the Bible,* 5 vols. (Grand Rapids: Zondervan, 1975), IV, 360–66.

our bedroom and proceeded up the stairs on all fours, thereby being miraculously delivered from a mop and handle on which hung a full bucket of water over the stairwell. As my hands pulled my tired body up the stairs past the lurking, but missed, trap, I emerged into the upper hallway to see thirteen surprised freshmen frozen in suspended motion. There were balloons, some collapsed and some still full all over the hall. Water was running off the ceiling, walls, and the fellows as if they had all just been in a downpour. "Gentlemen," I blurted out, "Who did this?" (That must be the most inept question I ever asked). "Yes," chimed in all thirteen men with mock sincerity, "Who did this?" "Did you?" "Did you?" "Did you?" Since they were Christians, they knew better than to lie; besides it was evident that they all must have been involved. Not one of them ever owned up to the deed, but I did get an illustration from the mess and the loss of sleep. So every time I read Malachi's audience replying, "Who us? We did this?" I sense again my own frustration when I faced those thirteen men who pretended to be just as indignant as I was over the results of their water fight. They pretended that they had no idea how all that water got there. They pretended to be hurt that I felt they could have done anything like that. It was no different for Malachi. "Who us?" they queried, "We would never despise God's name."

Malachi, however, is prepared to give an illustration of their despising God's name. They had belittled God's mighty person when they placed "polluted food on the altar" (v. 7). Frequently sacrifices were labeled by metonomy "bread" or "food" of God (e.g., Lev. 21:6,8,17,21,22; 22:25; Num 28:2).

The pollution was twofold. First, polluted men and women cannot offer pure sacrifices to God while they simultaneously reject his lordship and fail to glorify and enjoy him. It has always been a matter of priorities when we worship the living God. Our God inspects the *offerer* first and then his or her *offering*. He looks at my heart first, and then at my message, my solo, my offering. If it would not burden the ushers too much, this word could be paraphrased: "Put yourselves in the offering plate first and then deposit your offering for God." Even though the injunction is unrealistic, the level of priorities is correct, and has been since the first act of worship and first offerings brought by Cain and Abel. God inspects men's hearts before he looks at what they have brought in their hands.

Cain came to God because it was time to come while Abel came bringing some of the firstlings of the flock and the choicest pieces. Surprisingly, the text of Genesis 4 does not concentrate on the differences in the substance of the sacrifice, or on the altar, blood, smoke, or knife. None of these is ever raised in the text, which instead focuses on the men. With painful emphasis the Hebrew text of Genensis 4:3–4 says "Cain, he, he also, he brought" and "Abel, he, he also, he brought." Four elements stress the man: his proper name followed by the personal pronoun, an adverb, and a verb with the personal pronominal ending on it. Said the text again pointedly, "And the Lord had respect (note the verb which is used of persons mainly) for Abel *and* for his offering (apparently in that order), but for Cain *and* for his offering (again, note the order) he did not have respect" (the verb is still the one used of persons, 4:4*b*–5*a*). So polluted offerers can defile every single act of devotion, service, gift, and praise offered to God.

The gifts also can be polluted by virtue of the fact that they were blemished and not the choicest that could be given to God. When God asked for that which pictured his own sacrifice in all of his holiness and sinlessness, these priests insisted on lowering the standards, excusing the people and themselves for one reason or another. "Times are bad now," they might have said. "Economic conditions have still not been normalized ever since the Babylonian exile. We have all been badly hurt. These things take time, you know. It's best to take whatever little thing the people bring rather than be fussy or particular."

But such action was a defiling of God himself—note how they ask, "How have we defiled *you?*" They knew that what they did ultimately was directed against God himself. It was also a demeaning and belittling of the "table" (=altar; cf. Ps. 23:5; Ezek, 44:16) of God. Everything the sacrifical system stood for was being desecrated and dismantled at the hands of those who had pledged to serve God without fear or favor of men. They had made God's altar "despicable," a strong term indeed used to describe the Syrian king, Antiochus Epiphanes's desecration of the altar of God with a sow in 165 B.C. (Dan. 11:21). Such action simply did not ring true with their high sounding profession of God's fatherhood and lordship.

In Our Gifts (1:8–9)

Our Lord judges a gift by what the gift costs the offerer who placed it on the altar rather than by its intrinsic worth.[5] In these verses we are faced with a call to be real, authentic, and credible—men and women worthy of that love which has been so bountifully showered on us. But the area in which we are now challenged is the area of our gifts and giving.

The prophet must now attack the shame of placing on the altar something, but something that is basically valueless. It means little to us, and therefore it will mean little to God.

Already, Malachi has made it clear that polluted men cannot offer to God pure sacrifices. Authenticity can only come from a genuine heart and a prior interior commitment of one's self to the living Lord. Otherwise the pollution of our heart and hands infects everything we say and do.

There is a type of profanity that goes beyond cursing and swearing falsely—yes, even in our world where profanity of the lips has become such an ordinary means for expressing oneself. The profanity of our text exceeds others because it pretends to be an orthodoxy of form and words while the heart and eyes are heterodox and turned away from God. Thus, it is plain that our lives can pollute our professions, gifts, services, worship— indeed, all that we do. Our prayer ought to be, "Lord God, make me genuine and cleanse my polluted attitude, heart, and will. Make me your clean vessel so that not only what I say and bring to you, but also what I am, do, and believe may reflect a prior work of grace in my life by the help of your Holy Spirit."

We are called to probe a second area where a credibility gap

---

5. See G. Campbell Morgan, *Malachi's Message for Today* (Grand Rapids: Baker Book House, 1972 [reprint]), pp. 48–50 for the development of this idea.

exists. Once again the problem is one of violating sacred things, especially by those who were called to set the spiritual tone for Israel—his priests.

It was not that Israel or her priests had failed to give anything to God. That was not so. They were givers! No one could accuse them of being stingy and tightfisted, unresponsive and heartless in their giving to the needs of God's work. They gave all right, but they chose to give leftovers. They gave what was blind, lame, and sick. It had very little value in their eyes, and so they handed it over to God—as Westerners might today in order to get at least some government tax-credit for the gift. But then how could that gift have any value to God when it was offered both by a polluted person and represented only tokenism since the animal could render very little, if any more service to the one who gave it?

Giving something that costs us little or nothing is only another indication of phony religion. Surely, our estimate of God, his work, and his action in our present world will rise no higher than the value of the staggering, diseased animal we bring to the door of the house of God.

With biting irony, Malachi suggests that the same action be adopted when paying one's taxes to the state. See how pleased that makes your governor or ruler. Chances are that few would have the nerve to do such an audacious thing. Imagine someone writing to the local or national bureau of taxes and saying in effect,

> Dear Sir,
>
> Please accept this sick cow in lieu of the taxes I owe you. I trust that the old 'bag' recovers and will prove more useful to you than she has been to me. Frankly, I just can't spare anything more than this at the present time.
>
> Oh yes, please look after those requests that I made. I trust you will be able to improve our local roads and upgrade the quality of our education.   Sincerely,

Would the government stand for such action? Well, then, why should God—especially since he is a "great King" (v. 14, cf. vv. 5 and 11). The ruler of heaven and earth, oftentimes, gets treated more miserably than any human potentate ever would tolerate!

The law had required that the sacrificial victim be free from any kind of blemish and healthy in every particular (Exod. 12:5; 29:1; Lev. 1:3,10; 22:18–25; Num. 6:14; 19:2; Deut. 15:21; 17:1; Ezek. 45:23). Therefore, to violate this provision not only reflected the slight regard that the donor placed on his act, but also reflected his willingness to disobey the commandments of God and indicated in what contempt he held the picture of his own means of redemption. A blemished substitute could never depict the sacrifice of the Lord Jesus, which every atoning sacrifice in the Old Testament anticipated. It was a direct insult to the gift that was to provide eternal life for all who would believe, even in Old Testament times. It was an act of sacrilege to offer the blind, lame, and sick. Not only was it valueless; it also was blasphemous— especially when Leviticus 22:18–25 and Deuteronomy 15:21 expressly forbade offering blemished animals. Is it not evil? asks Malachi (1:8). How could anyone put God off with such shreds and mediocre remnants of their substance, gifts, and strength?

But who had encouraged such indolence? Was it not a kind of discount religion fostered by the priests of God (v. 9)—perhaps in a move to involve more people? Malachi lashes out in bitter sarcasm against these cut-rate priests and urged them to go now, on the basis of such paltry worship of God, and pray for these same persons that God would grant them their every request. "See now if God will hear either your prayer or theirs," seems to be the challenge of the prophet.

Since the worshipers, encouraged by a grossly indifferent priesthood, had violated both the reverence for God's altar (with their polluted verbal professions and hearts) and now reverence for the Lord himself, there was little chance that God would be disposed to hear anyone's prayer or grant their requests. "Supplicate (or literally, 'make smooth' [if you now can]) the face of God" (v. 9; cf. the same expression in Zech. 7:2). He deliberately used the name "El" instead of the personal name of the God who would be there, Yahweh, in order to stress the great gap that exists between a human governor and the incomparably great Creator of the universe, Elohim.

The tragedy of this whole affair was that it had all been perpetrated by God's delegated ministers, his priests: "From your hands" has this [i.e., indulging the people by accepting any old

animal for sacrifice] proceeded (v. 9b). Such a ragtag lot of
sacrificial animals should never be accepted for worship. The
tone of this passage is not a call to repentance, but is an ironical castigation for such abusive permissiveness. Besides, gifts
offered to God could never be the basis for securing his favor
(Ps. 40:6–8).

There is a great deal of sacrificial giving from the believing
household of faith and evangelicals. But there is also an enormous
amount of sacrilegious giving which has indulged itself in dedicating to God what modern men and women could spare or what
was left over after they had sought all their own pleasure and
projects. Is this not the same thing as dedicating to God's service
what is of little or no value?

How is it that the widow whom Jesus praised in Luke 21:3 "gave
more than they all [gave]"? When a few pence outweigh more
than all the large coins from a whole stream of givers, we have
either a form of new math or a spiritual principle. Since we cannot
justify a new type of arithmetic here, we conclude that our Lord
measures our gifts first by inspecting the heart and person of the
giver and then by what it cost the giver who presented it. Surely,
that is the theology that also lies behind this section of Malachi.

In Our Service (1:10–12)

Verses 10–12 introduce a third area where we are called to be
authentic: in our services. Once again, it is the priests who are
directly confronted with the challenge; but the rest of the believing community is never far from view, especially since verse 14
clearly expands the address to include everyone.

So distasteful were the unauthorized sacrifices permitted by
the priests that Malachi now makes an outrageous suggestion:
lock the double doors of the temple court and block all access to
the altar of God! Such a lamentable action was preferable to the
hideous perpetuation of worthless worship. No worship at all is
better than cold and negligent worship of God. It would be
blasphemous to continue to palm off such ridiculous insults to
the high God.

In a bold move the prophet intones:

"Oh, that one of you would shut the temple doors, so that you would not light useless fires on my altar! I am not pleased with you," says the LORD Almighty, "and I will accept no offering from your hands." (1:10 NIV)

This ironical suggestion was to dramatize graphically how things had deteriorated. How shocking it would be to see God's house boarded up with a large sign over it, Closed! Out of Business. "Scandalous. A sure sign of a decadent society," many would be sure to say.

But was it any better with the pretense continuing? The God who began this prophecy pledging "I have loved you" (1:2) dared to tell it like it was because his people were imperiling their own lives in perpetuating such a humdrum worship. Therefore, let someone with the fortitude and gumption close the whole charade down. Such mediocre, lackluster, lifeless type of worship and service was a bother to God and to man. Shut the doors and nail them closed. Let the facts speak for themselves to a watching world.

One other suggestion, urges Malachi, will match this state of affairs: let someone with enough courage and audacity see to it that no one lights a fire on the altar *in vain*. The Hebrew word for "in vain" appears thirty-two times in the Old Testament and generally means "for no reason, without a cause."

These unauthorized and worthless sacrifices were profaning God's holy name. They were not offered with the purpose and goal that God had in mind, hence they were useless. Thus God's holy name was appealed to in a worthless and objectless way. The whole exercise became vain repetition and only magical in a cultic way. But when men and women begin to offer to God and worship him by rote in an unthinking, unthankful way, they besmirch the holiness of his person and great name.

There is, unfortunately, a bland kind of Christian belief which is without object, purpose, or goal. It is perfunctory, dull, and exeedingly vapid and empty. For such paltry gifts and vacuous service, religion is futile, despite the verbal protestations to the contrary. It will not amount to anything. Stop it. Shut up the house of God permanently; stop the acts of worship and remove the symbols of fellowship between God and man. It is all hypocrisy and pretense.

On this point Malachi (and perhaps my reader) has had enough of negativism. Like a funeral dirge or the boom of one cannon report after another, the indictments have been hammered home one after the other. Some will explain, "But that is because this is the Old Testament" (with emphasis and a long hold on the word *ooolldd*).

But we are surprised and pleased to find that the bad news is suddenly replaced by an inbursting of good news in Malachi 1:11.[6] Even the introductory words are meant to surprise us, for the verse begins with the particle of asseveration meaning "yes, indeed." So an unexpected truth, which will now transcend the paltry inadequacies of a fainthearted priesthood or stingy populace, is interjected so that the listener or reader will not become discouraged and conclude that God is perhaps powerless to rescue his holy name.

Such an abrupt intrusion is not unusual for Old Testament writers. Frequently, even in the midst of a list of curses and judgments, there will come dramatic relief lifting the heart like a burst of glorious sunshine after many dreary days of overcast weather. That is what happened in Genesis 3:15 and Hosea 13:14 (the latter became the basis for Paul's famous taunt to death in 1 Cor. 15:54).

But if the text bursts into our consciousness with a rush of excitement, it is sustained beyond the introductory word with a message that boggles the mind with the universality of its claims and the height to which it exalts the name of the Lord. The living Lord is just not going to allow this constant despising of his name and the pollution of his altar to continue. The fact of the matter is, he will triumph, and he can and will raise up true worship and worshipers to his name from around the globe. The only question is whether those who presently are called by his name and who have found the worship of his person so tedious will be part of that great host. So never fear, warns our text: God's righteous

6. Peter A. Verhoef, "Some Notes on Malachi 1:11," in *Proceedings of the Ninth Meeting of* Die Ou-Testamentiese Werkgemeenskap in Suid-Afrika, (Stellenbosch: University of Stellenbosch, 1966), pp. 163–72.

servant will have success. He is not saddled with Israel or with contemporary conservatives, evangelicals, or whatever other privileged group some may feel they belong to.

The geographic, political, and ethnic scope of this promise is set forth immediately. It will be from "the rising of the sun to its setting." Four other times in the Old Testament similar terminology is used to depict the universality of God's reign (Pss. 50:1; 113:3; Isa. 45:6, 59:19) when he will disclose himself as Creator, Redeemer, and King. This clause is elucidated in a parallel clause, "in every place." The sweep of God's success will be from East to West. The vastness of this territory far exceeds any mere territory of Israel. In fact, his name will be "great among the nations," or Gentiles. Now there is an explosive theme. Who would ever have believed a thing like that could happen? Of course, Malachi had already hinted at such a state of affairs when he affirmed in 1:5: "Great is the LORD, beyond the border of Israel!" And verse 14 confirmed the correctness of this translation by adding: "for I am a great King, says the LORD of hosts, and my name will be feared among the nations [or Gentiles]."

Had not Israel been called to be "a kingdom of priests" and a "light to the nations" (Isa. 42:6; 49:6)?[7] Had she not been told that in her seed "all the nations of the earth would be blessed" (Gen. 12:3)? Had God not purposed to bless "all the ends of the earth" (Ps. 67) in exactly the same words we know as the Aaronic benediction from Numbers 6:24–26? His announcement of his universal lordship should not have surprised the people in 400 B.C.

If the scope of this exciting word encompassed all nations, languages, and political units, East and West, then the idea that those who once were mere heathen could offer sacrifices pleasing to God, vis á vis the odious pretense that Israel was currently living out—that was a bombshell! But had not the prophets anticipated the conversion of the nations? (Cf. Isa. 2:2–4; 11:10; 55:3–5; 66:18–21; Ezek. 36:23; 37:28; 38:23; and 39:7: "the nations will know that I am the Lord").

7. See Walter C. Kaiser, Jr., "Israel's Missionary Call," in *Perspectives on the World Christian Movement: A Reader*, ed. Ralph D. Winter and Steven C. Hawthorne, (Pasadena: William Carey Library, 1981), pp. 25–34.

Impure, reluctant service will be exceeded by the pure, acceptable worship that shall come up to God from the peoples all over
the earth (note the contrast between the nations, Mal. 1:11, and
"but you" in v. 12). The offerings these nations give would be
"pure." In terms of the law of Leviticus 11 or Deuteronomy
14:3–19, an offering was pure when the animal was without
blemish and offered as the law prescribed. The usual Hebrew
adjective for "without blemish" is not used here; it is a word that
involves one's moral and physical purity as well as the usual
ceremonial purity. How then could pagans offer such "pure"
sacrifices, given the moral standards of Israel's pagan neighbors?
This was all too much to comprehend.

It is not that the nations already were in reality worshiping the
Lord, when they offered sacrifice to their gods who were but other
names for Yahweh! This view was popularized by such early
church fathers as Justin, Irenaeus, Clement of Alexandria, Theodore of Mopsuestia, and Augustine. But Malachi would reject
such a line of argument, for he is talking about pure sacrifices and
ones offered to Yahweh's *name*. Moreover, while it was already
possible for Gentiles to be part of God's family of believers (note
the present tense in vv. 5 and 14 "I *am* a great King" and "My name
is feared among the nations"), still the passive participle can be
(and here probably should be) translated as a future (Gen. 15:14;
Joel 3:4; 2 Sam. 20:21;[8] verse 11 anticipated sometime in the
future).

The incense offered no doubt reflects the altar of incense with
the symbol of its sweet aroma of the prayers of the saints (cf. Rev.
5:8) constantly going up before God (cf. a close Hebrew form for
"incense" in Exod. 30:1). The amazing revelation, however, is that
it would be offered "in every place", not just the temple. That must
have startled all who first heard it. How could that be? Was not the
offering of incense the sole prerogative of the high priest (Num.
16)? How then could it be offered in "every place"—unless some
other bizarre thing was planned such as letting the Gentiles offer
it for themselves all over the world!

Others have attempted to write off these verses as references to

8. See the references and arguments of Balwin, *Haggai, Zechariah, and Malachi*, p. 229,
n. 1.

the Jews of the Dispersion (Rashi or the Jews of Justin Martyr's time, *Dialogue with Trypho*, 117). There is a small element of truth in this view, but it hardly meets the demand of the whole text. The offerings here are more than incense and grain; they apply to all offerings, including meat. Moreover, they are "pure." One could say that the reference is also to Gentile proselytes, with all nations being represented by individual believers at that time. While partially true, it hardly complies with the terms of our text, and we have too little knowledge of Malachi's day to affirm the state of proselyte believers.

If the Jewish diaspora and Gentile proselytism already signaled the firstfruits, the full harvest anticipated in these verses was yet to come. (Cf. Isa. 11:10; 66:20; Zeph. 2:11; Zech. 9:10). This text then carries us from what was begun in Malachi's day, as a sort of harbinger of things to come, to the messianic age. The fact that offerings can be offered everywhere on earth, not just in Jerusalem, and that all believers, not just priests in the temple, are offering sacrifices accords with two facts presented elsewhere. (1) The truth presented to the Samaritan woman at the well of Sychar (John 4:20–23): "You say that in Jerusalem is the place where men ought to worship." Jesus said to her, "neither on this mountain nor in Jerusalem will you worship the Father. . . . But the hour is coming, and now is, when the true worshipers will worship the Father in spirit and truth" (cf. also Exod. 20:24 "in every place"). (2) The idea that the priestly function, which originally belonged to all members of the covenant people in the time of the patriarchs and the promise of Exodus 19:5–6, will be accorded also to the Gentiles (Isa. 66:21, "And some of them [Gentiles] also I will take for priests and for Levites, says the LORD").

No wonder Malachi twice promises "My name will be great among the nations." The middle wall of partition will be destroyed (Eph. 2:14) and God's kingdom will be set up over the whole earth.

In contrast to this marvelous interlude with its happy assurance of the triumph of God everywhere, there is the mediocre service of the priests of Malachi's day, "But you" (v. 12). The complaint of the priests was that they just couldn't help it. It was the altar. People just didn't go for that stuff anymore. "It's the altar, not us," they complained. "We are living in changing times, and the altar and the fruit or produce on it, i.e., the sacrifices are contemptible." Like the sons of Eli, the priests decided to change the law of the sacrifice on their own. Their charge is, in part, a revival of the argument in verse 7.

The complaint of the priests was not as some have thought, that their work was too heavy while their remuneration was too light, i.e., the "food" counting in this interpretation, as the portion that fell to the priests. Nor was it that the food was from blind, lame, or sick animals, since they would have no one but themselves to blame for such permissiveness. The problem, rather, was the indifference and carelessness of the priests in what they were willing to accept on God's behalf. Furthermore, when challenged and "caught" in the act of lowering God's standards, they tried to shift the blame from themselves to the act of sacrifice itself and to the prescribed food or content of the sacrifice. In other words, "It is sacrifices and those prescribed animals, not us, that you should be objecting to," chorused Malachi's audience.

How easy it is to shift the blame from ourselves to others or to things. There is no end to rationalizing and explaining away what we do not wish to face, but oh how false and boring is that service.

Meanwhile, God is able to raise up a people to take our place in serving him if we persist in wishing to serve him half-heartedly. That is not the service that befits the great King or a redeemed people.

In Our Time 1:13–14

Boredom had to be the outcome of such hypocritical ministry for one whom the priests claimed was their Father and their Lord and Master. The fourth and final area in which the probing word of God issued a call for authenticity in that ancient culture and in ours is that of time.

Sooner or later the tedium and emptiness had to lead to a begrudging of the very time involved in the service and worship of God. This boredom could be spotted in three different areas: (1) their words, (2) their spirit or attitudes, and (3) their deeds.

Their words told the whole story: "Behold, what a weariness!"

No longer was it a joy—if it ever was for these distraught priests—to care for the ritual and offerings. It was a drudgery and a burden. Only the necessity of appearances kept them at it all. But the dull routine was not verbalized. "Religious services are a bore and we no longer get anything from them," they echoed each other. Their work was a nuisance and they hated it.

Their spirit agreed with this assessment. Haughtily, they sniffed at this whole troublesome affair. Their contempt for religious service knew no end. Now they showed public contempt by pretending to be above the issue and the trouble or burden of the altar and what was on it.

One final stroke made their lives a consistent witness. They too brought to God's altar what had been stolen, was lame or sick. What more convincing evidence could be given for a lackluster experience of their spiritual deadness? The only question was the Lord's: "Should I receive *that* from your hand? Emphatically not! And if it was so totally unacceptable, then why bring it in the first place?"

The robbery of sacrificial animals was not mentioned in Malachi 1:8. But the practice was prevalent enough to earn Isaiah's rebuke: "I hate robbery for the burnt offering" (61:8). Herbert Wolf notes that this word used for robbery is linked with oppressing widows and orphans in Job 24:3 and Isaiah 10:2.[9] If that is how the gift to God was obtained, how could God bless it? Sacrifice that costs us nothing could not be claimed as a sacrifice.

The final verse of the chapter is joined to verse 13 by a simple copula, "and." It attaches to the expected answer of no for the question posed in verse 13b a curse on every Israelite, not just the priests, who dares to offer blemished or stolen animals to God.

To have vowed to give a male animal, as specified in Leviticus 22:19, or an unblemished animal in thanksgiving to God for delivering them (cf. Gen. 28:20–22; Num. 30:2) and then suddenly to substitute a cheap imitation for the same was to swindle or cheat God. All the while, the offerer owned the proper animal that was required in both instances. The deceit in what was optional and voluntary made it all the more incongruous. The whole affair

9. Herbert Wolf, *Haggai and Malachi: Rededication and Renewal* (Chicago: Moody Press, 1976), p. 76.

was totally inexcusable. Only a desire to be something in public that one was not in one's own heart could have led to this type of showmanship. This man wanted to be known as a spiritual person and so he voluntarily vowed one thing, but gave another. This was no more acceptable than the deceit pulled by Ananias and Sapphira (Acts 5:1–5). God will have no part of such men or their tricky sacrificial vows.

It is because God is the great King whose name, reputation, characteristics, and doctrines will be known and revered among all the nations. The theme of the incomparable greatness of God is explored in two great teaching passages: Psalm 139 and Isaiah 40, in addition to many briefer notices to this same theme. The question is: "To whom [or to what], then, shall we liken him or make him equal?" A thousand times over should come the answer: "There is no one like unto you."

Any such cheap, shabby treatment of a mere human monarch would have easily aroused his anger and wrath. What, then of the King of kings? God's kingship must never be lost sight of, for if we are his subjects and sons our behavior ought to reflect the same. The fact that God is king has frequent notices in Scripture: 1 Samuel 12:12, "The LORD your God was your king"; Psalm 10:16, "The LORD is king for ever and ever"; Psalm 24:8, "Who is the King of glory? The LORD, strong and mighty, the LORD, mighty in battle!"; Psalm 84:3, "O LORD of hosts, my King and my God"; Psalm 95:3, "For the LORD is a great God, and a great King above all gods"; and frequently in the prophets (Isa. 33:22; 43:15; 44:6, Jer. 8:19; 10:10; Zeph. 3:15).[10]

The present age has men by the scores who have concluded that the church and its clerical ministry is a weariness. Their own hearts condemn them, and they have decided to quit.

But is not the problem just as acute in the pew? Is it not a joy for men and women of the twentieth century to sit through a three- to four-hour opera or symphony (and it should be) or to attend a marathon sports event and rejoice when the game goes into extra innings or periods. But these same people may fidget and gripe when the allotted time for divine worship of God runs over! Will our Lord accept such obvious boredom? Shall we continue to hire

---

10. This list may be found in Smith, *Commentary on the Book of Malachi*, pp. 34–35.

professional singers and musicians and reward them, at least on the American scene, with a check for $500 to $2500 for a single performance and then begrudge $25 for a guest sermon? People, they say, don't go for preaching much these days; they must be entertained. Is this not another evidence of a shift in values? The public reading of Scripture has gone too far, for many, when more than ten verses are read from God's Holy Word, but our capacity is easily tripled and more when we turn on the television set, open our favorite newsmagazine or newspaper, or settle down to a novel.

Can we continue to claim the status of sons? Where then is his honor? Can we loudly protest that our God is our Lord and Master if we do not revere him?

It is not he, but we who need to be credible. We must become more authentic and real in our profession, our gifts, our service, and our time—especially since he is the great King and his name will be great among all the nations of the earth.

3

A Call to Love God Totally
(Malachi 2:1-16)

The prophet had turned aside momentarily to challenge the people in Malachi 1:14, but now he returns to the priests and the ministry itself. Every part of this passage is capable of being applied to the Christian ministry and to God's people at large, for it deals, not with the priest's sacrificial duties, but with their teaching role, their regard for God's people, and their treatment of their wives.

The reminders in this text are quite stern, for failure to be authentic and true to the Scripture is not a slight offense in a teaching opportunity. Whenever the teacher of God's word causes people who are seeking the truth to stumble or whenever that teacher fails to warn of the impending wrath of God because of disobedience, then a special judgment falls on that teacher. Thus verses 4-9 are at the heart of the loves espoused here.

But even prior to that task is the aim and focus of all our emotions and actions toward God. We must make it our ambition to bring glory to God, and that glory will only come when we seek to honor him as Lord in every aspect of our lives. What is true of all men and women is especially or doubly true for the Christian ministry. We must make it our aim to please him (cf. 2 Cor. 5:9), and that is what Malachi 2:2 also urges as the aim of all ministry.

Thus the concern for the glory of God and the Word of God lead off in Malachi 2. Anything less than a full-hearted response to the honor, reputation, and status of the living God and the truth taught in his Word is a type of moral pollution. It is a substitution of something ephemeral, transitory, unsatisfying, and spiritually empty of nutritional value for something abiding, substantial, and nourishing to the total being of individuals.

But this chapter raises three other obstacles to the spiritual unity that should characterize God's people, viz, mixed marriages, unfaithfulness in marriage, and the issue of divorce. Each of these actions is an act of treachery; a masking of the commonality that should be evident had those of Malachi's day—and we ourselves —been totally loving God with heart, soul, and mind.

This text, then, calls for four new *affections* (our homiletical keyword) if we are to respond adequately to the Lord whose ringing declaration of his persistent love for us continues to resound from the opening of the Book of Malachi, " 'I have loved you,' says the Lord." Thus, four affections may be grouped in this manner:

> Love for God's glory—2:1-3
>
> Love for God's Word—2:4-9
>
> Love for God's people—2:10-12
>
> Love for God's gift of a marriage partner—2:13-16

Each passage revolves around a central idea in the sections singled out in the pattern noted above. In verses 1-3, verse 2 urges us (to put the matter in its positive form) to "lay it to heart to give glory to [God's] name" while verses 4-9 center on verse 7, "The lips of a priest should guard knowledge, and men should seek instruction from his mouth, for he is the messenger of the LORD of hosts." The last two sections continue the theme, but are more closely related when verses 10-12 ask, not the priests in particular, but all the people, "Have we not all one father?" (v. 10) and verse 15, "Has not the one God made [one, i.e., wife for each man]", even though he had the residue of the Spirit to [make more than one]?" Let none be faithless to the wife of his youth.

Malachi's sweep of the issues is mind-boggling in its intensity, scope, and ability to probe and root out problems so central and determinative for many other issues that we are at once startled by their sheer simplicity and also by their profundity. This is another revolutionary summons to a wholly different type of lifestyle that moves majestically from a love for the glory of God and the instruction found in his Word to a love for the whole company of the people of God and for that partner we vowed before God and witnesses to love and cherish until death separated us. Seldom do we see such grand scope in so few verses in the Biblical text.

Love for God's Glory (2:1-3)

The rebuke of Malachi 1:6-14 is now followed by the threat of punishment that would be a foregone conclusion if the priests did not repent. As with all of God's threats issued before the point of no return has been passed, this one also carried with it a hopeful condition, "if." This word came as a sort of ultimatum, or as the translations phrase verse 1, a "command." Since there is no express "command" in the immediate context, it is the "decision," "resolution," or "decree" (see Nahum 1:14 for a similar use) faced by the priests. Will they respond to this injunction to honor and glorify God, or will they refuse to take it to heart? The idiom to "lay it to heart" is a call for some serious thought and action.

It cannot be emphasized too frequently that God's love for his people dominates this book. Malachi 1:2 functions like a banner for each section of this prophecy: "I have loved you, says the LORD." The witness of his love in the announced threat of judgment can even be seen in the "if" of verse 2.

The "name" of God appears now for the sixth time in the first sixteen verses of Malachi (1:6, 11 (three times), 14; 2:2). That name is the summation of all that God is in his person, character, reputation, doctrine, and ethical instruction.[1] God's name had been despised by the shabbiness and heartlessness of an inauthentic profession and service of God at his altar (1:6). How could the priests invoke the gracious name of God over the people as Numbers 6:24-26 had laid out, when they themselves were largely responsible for blocking out the blessings of God?

The chief end of the priests of Malachi's day was—and of the

---

1. See discussion of the "name" in Mal. 1:6, p. 33; 36–7 above.

Christian ministry of our day still is—to glorify God. They, as is
true of all God's people, were to give glory to God's name above
every other name. In Hebrew the word for "glory" spoke first of the
weight, the sheer gravity of his presence. It was that weight of
presence which defined his importance and the respect he
inspired. Thus glory was not so much the renown as the real
value a person carried because of who he was and what he did.
Accordingly, for the priests to give glory to God meant sanctifying,
or setting apart as separate and altogether different in being and
essence, the person of the living God, in their service to him and
in their lives. In a wider sense, it meant holding high the reality of
God's presence in their lives accompanied by high praise, honor,
and adoration. In practical terms it meant seeking first his reign,
rule, and righteousness before all other loves and goals in life
(Matt. 6:33). So it should ever be for all of God's people.

Whatever failed to measure up to this aim for life and ministry
was empty and hollow. It was accepting the "form of godliness" in
place of the power found in the real goal of living and serving our
Lord (cf. 2 Tim. 3:5). It was professing that God was known
personally even while works denied the fact (Titus 1:16).

The threat, "I will send the curse on you" (Mal. 2:2) is almost an
exact quotation from Deuteronomy 28:20; a passage, together with
Leviticus 26, which offered the alternative prospect of blessing or
judgment, depending on how God's people lived and responded
to his Word. Another link between Malachi 2:2-3 and Deuteronomy 28:20 was the word "rebuke," which occurred as a verb
in Malachi, but as a noun in Deuteronomy.[2] It is this observation
that helps us to explain the clause in verse 3: "I will rebuke your
seed;" for while "seed" often relates to one's offspring, its connection with Deuteronomy 28 tilts the evidence in favor of the
produce that comes from the ground (note the context of Deut.
28:18-19, 21, 23-24). To rebuke the seed is to stop its growth.

The penalty for the leader's failure to hear and to respond is
stern. Three times the text mentions a curse that God would bring
for such unbelief and disobedience. God's name is serious business, and nothing pollutes it more than the misconduct of those
whose business is to honor it. But our God loves us so faithfully

---

2. As observed by Herbert Wolf, *Haggai and Malachi,* p. 79.

that when we refuse to be taught by *precept*, he will continue by that same love to pursue us by *penalty* until we are driven back to his loving embrace once again. God will curse our blessings, i.e., he will send a curse and a destruction upon that which we count as our blessing.

Our blessings are all our gifts, goods,[3] and even the words promising both (Num. 6:24-26). In fact, *already* the judgment of God had begun, and this was an added incentive to act in light of the certainty of what was taking place. The repetition of the words at the end of verse 2 was not, as some have contended,[4] superfluous. Instead, it underscored the generous nature of God's grace by repeating once again the substance of the protasis and apodosis.

The fact that the seed, i.e., the crops, could be affected by man's sin again points out the close relationship that exists by divine appointment between the soil, including all of nature, and man's spiritual progress, or lack thereof. God made man from the dust of the earth in Genesis 2:7. But Adam and Eve sinned, and because of this close tie with the soil and because the acme of creation was invested in mankind, the dirt was adversely affected (Gen. 3:17-19). Accordingly, it may be observed that whenever there is a general turning away from God in a nation or community, there often is an effect on the crops and the productivity of the natural world. So real is this linkage, not only in Genesis 3, but also currently, and especially in the *eschaton*, that Paul notes the whole created order, along with us, continues to groan in travail up to the present moment waiting on tiptoes, as it were, for the final work of redemption at the second coming of Christ (Rom. 8:22-23). Is it any wonder, then, that Malachi 2:3 threatens a reluctant priesthood with crop failure and a downturn in agricultural productivity unless they repent?

The disgrace of such gross sins committed by the serving ministry of the land is introduced into what was basically a farm culture. The dung, and perhaps the entrails, of the animals which remained after the sacrifices had been performed would be smeared on the faces of the priests. The poetic justice in this fair

---

3. Smith, in *Commentary on the Book of Malachi*, p. 36, notes that in Ethiopic "blessings" often means "goods" as in Mal. 3:10; Gen. 49:25f, Pss. 21:3; 84:5-6; Prov. 28:20; Isa. 65:8.

4. E.g., Smith, ibid.

turnabout of events which were done with such hypocrisy can be captured by our idiom that the priests would be left with egg on their faces! Everyone would begin to demean and to belittle them and the priesthood in general. The ministry would be held up to contempt, scorn, and mocking jokes because people would place little stock in such transparently false worship.

Even more damaging was the last line of verse 3. The priests would be separated and removed from the presence of the living God. Like refuse, i.e., the dung, flesh, hide, and entrails of the sacrifices (cf. Lev. 8:17; 16:27), they too would be placed outside the camp and away from the *Shekinah*, presence of God. How dearly must these priests—and those who serve in the ministry today—pay should they refuse to make it their aim to bring glory to God's name. The effects would be felt, not only in the demise of esteem for their office and person, but also on the very productivity of the land itself.

Pretentiousness is so artificial, especially where spiritual matters are involved. But God would take some of the very materials left from the sacrifices and would make the scent of the indignities and insults handed out by the clergy as permanent on these men of the cloth as was the refuse and dung left from those same sacrifices that ordinarily would be safely removed outside the camp and burned.

Love for God's Word (2:4-9)

The invitation for the priests to desist from their refusal to give God glory had been more than a hypothetical anticipation of what could go wrong. The fact of the matter was that already it was possible to contrast the wretched state of affairs in the contemporary priesthood with some of the faithful priests of the past. The culpable conduct of the ungodly priests of Malachi's day made it all the more imperative that they realize that "this commandment," the threatened punishment of verses 2-3, was real if they did not cease from their present course of life. In fact, it was given so that the priesthood might continue. Their laxness and indifference to the ceremonial and moral aspects of their faith had aroused the anger of God to such a point that God's covenant with Levi was put in jeopardy.

The expression in Malachi 2:4 is an elliptical construction. But overall, this is its sense: The commandment was sent so that, by taking it to heart, the Levitical priesthood might continue. The judgment, sentence, decree (all alternate senses for "commandment") had to come, should they not respond to the conditional offer, so that "you will know" that the Lord's word once again was true and dependable. This phrase, "you will know [that I am the Lord]" regularly occurs in texts where the judgment of God was used as a lever to help men and women face up experientially to the claims of who this God is and what men and women must do in believing response (cf. the experience of Pharaoh and the Egyptians in Exod. 7:10[14]; 9:14, 29-30; 10:2; 14:2,18; or others in Ezek. 15:7; 33:29).

"Levi" here is used in the sense of the Levitical priesthood. It is not the specific son of Jacob that is in view, but the whole priestly class as represented by Levi. Malachi prefers to refer to the priests as "sons of Levi" (Hebrew text 3:3) even though they are technically in the narrower class of Levites descended from the "sons of Aaron" (Lev. 8:1-4) or even later on, the "sons of Zadok" (Ezek. 44:15). This does not mean that Malachi was confused or that his designation antedated according to the nontraditional views of some, the time in Israel's history when, the priesthood was limited to Aaron's line in distinction to the more general work around the temple by all the other Levites. Malachi was well aware of the fact that it was Aaron's sons who were the priests, technically speaking. However, it was also possible to refer in a general sense to all who served around the temple as the priestly class, that is, the "sons of Levi."

God's covenant with Levi included "life and peace." Both the words and phraseology at once recall Numbers 25:12-13, where Yahweh established just such a covenant with Phinehas because he was aroused to action in the presence of the evil publicly flaunted by the Simeonite Zimri and the Midianite woman Cozbi. While the congregation was assembled in repentance and contrition before God, Zimri and Cozbi brazenly walked across the encampment to his tent to commit fornication in the name of religious prostitution and worship of the dead (Num. 25:6-8; Ps. 106:28-31). But Phinehas "stood up and interposed" (Ps. 106:30) and pierced both of them through while they were in the very act of cohabitation and "that was reckoned to him as righteousness" (Ps. 106:31) because he was "jealous with [God's] jealousy" (Num. 25:11). Consequently, God gave him this gift of peace which would be for him and his descendants after him, "a perpetual priesthood, because he was jealous for his God, and made atonement for the people of Israel" (Num. 25:13).

How different and direct was Phinehas' attitude in contrast with that of the priests of Malachi's day. He had feared God and "stood in awe of [God's] name" (Mal. 2:5), but where was that same fear among the sons of Levi now? asked in 1:6. The verb to "stand in awe" in 2:5 often occurs in this combination: "do not fear or be dismayed" (Deut. 1:21; Jer. 1:17).[5] The verb "to be dismayed" or even "shattered", as the nations were before God in Isaiah 8:9, is the same as "to stand in awe" here. "Do not fear or stand in awe" of men; rather, "fear and stand in awe" of God![6]

"Life and peace" (v. 5) were gifts that God gave to obedient men. Repeatedly, Deuteronomy and Proverbs urged that these blessings were the result of totally committing oneself to the commandments of God (e.g., Deut. 4:40; 6:2; 30:15-20; Prov. 3:1,2; 4:10,22; 6:23). Yahweh's gift was given so that Israel might not only have life, but have it more abundantly. Likewise, her peace included all her physical, spiritual, and economic welfare, viz, the quiet life, with health, protection, prosperity, and spiritual progress. At its heart, it was a message of peace because it began with men reconciled to God through faith in the messianic person who was to come. Even Phinehas experienced that peace in the turmoil that beset Israel through the trouble inaugurated by Balaam's malicious counsel (Num. 31:16; 2 Pet. 2:15; Rev. 2:14), for God's peace confronts sin and through his atonement, our peace is obtained. But alas, these priests knew nothing of that life or peace—and worse still, they robbed the people of the benefits of the same!

In contrast to the dismal record of these priests who had not feared God or stood in awe of his name, Malachi set forth the real task of the true servant of God. Those earlier worthies taught the truth and lived lives which were honoring to God (v. 6). The two aspects of word and life belonged together, for words are an index

5. As observed by Wolf, *Haggai and Malachi*, pp. 81-82.
6. Ibid.

to the character of the one who speaks them (Prov. 12:17-19; James 1:26; 3:2-12).

The aspects of the knowledge that was guarded and preserved on the lips of the priests were as follows:

It must be true (2:6a)

The exposition of the law must be in accordance with what it actually taught as indicated by the truth-intention of the human writer who stood in the counsel of God and first received that word. It has to be without any hint of self-seeking, partiality, or perverseness. Such preparation of the Word of God by teachers and pastors today will continue to take time in thoughtful and diligent study along with prayerful reflection and meditation. All too frequently the end is used to justify the means, which in this case often entails using some of the same worked-over truisms that more properly belong with better-known contexts rather than the ones that the teacher or expositor is allegedly teaching.

It must be bold (2:6b)

The proclaimer must not fear the faces or reproaches of the audience. It does not take long for a speaker to learn what an audience wishes to hear, but woe betide the speaker who compromises himself or the message in order to placate an audience when the Word of God has said otherwise!

It must turn men and women away from iniquity (2:6c)

Solid, faithful Biblical preaching will have as its aim the turning of sinners away from their sins. In its aftermath will come repentance of sin and faith toward God. Notice that the priesthood is envisioned as something more than a group of men who merely perform set functions connected with the prescribed ritual of the ceremonial law. Instead, they are men who also transmit the will of God. Their reward, like that in Daniel 12:3 is that they will "turn many to righteousness."

It must be impartial (2:9)

God's servants must not allow their teaching and their handling of people to be influenced by considerations of power, status, age, gifts, bribes, place, or anything similar. The reason for this injunction harks back to the theology of Deuteronomy 10:17 where the Lord our God is described as one "who is not partial and [who] takes no bribe[s]." To discriminate between rich and poor, young and old, the powerful and the powerless is to teach and administer in a way that will earn the rebuke of God and ultimately, the scorn of the populace when they too begin to see through the favoritism. It is all too easy to bend the message in favor of lobbies, committees, programs, organizations, feelings of special interest groups, or those with influence inside and outside the body of Christ.

But more than teaching the truth of the Word was involved here; there was also the matter of a corresponding faithfulness in lifestyle. In former days, the priests "walked with me," said the Lord, "in peace and uprightness" (Mal. 2:6c). To "walk with God" meant to live in full accord and harmony with the divine will. It denoted an even more intimate fellowship with God than did the more frequent expression to "walk after" God (e.g., Deut. 8:19; 13:4; 2 Kings 23:3; Jer. 7:9; Hos. 11:10). The phrase to "walk with" is used of two men in the OT and no others:[7] Enoch ("walked with God, and he was not, for God took him," Gen. 5:22,24) and Noah ("walked with God," 6:9). So the clause is used sparingly in Scripture and always of an extremely close communion, fellowship, worship, and life lived in the presence of God.

Malachi 2:7 enlarges on this dual mission of lip and life. The priests, like the Christian teacher or minister, was to preserve or "guard knowledge" by hiding it away in their hearts and minds. Psalm 119:11 urged, "I have hidden your word in my heart that I might not sin against you." And that knowledge of God had its roots in "the fear of the LORD" (Prov. 1:7)—a theme often alluded to in Malachi (cf. Hos. 4:1,6; 6:6). Men and women had a right to expect sound "instruction," thus all sloth in the thorough preparation of one's message was totally out of character for the servant of God.

The only time that a priest is called a "messenger of the LORD of hosts" is found in verse 7. In previous OT passages, this phrase

7. Consideration must also be given to Gen. 17:1 where the Lord said to Abraham, "I am (God Almighty) El Shaddai; walk before me, and be blameless."

normally represented the angel of the Lord, or even a Chris-
tophany.[8] Only in Haggai 1:13 is it a title also for a prophet; thus
the teaching ministry of the priesthood, as well as the more
traditional role of the prophet, was emphasized in this startling
title. Malachi will use this term "angel" or "messenger" to refer to
the forerunner of Christ, i.e., John the Baptist and to Christ himself
twice in 3:1.

It should also be noted that the priests were called upon to
exercise judicial functions in Deuteronomy 17:9-11 and 19:17. As
such, their job once again called for impartiality. This made the
accusation of partiality and showing favoritism in Malachi 2:9 all
the more heinous.

No wonder the gap between the standard set by those earlier
priests and the woeful inadequacies of the priesthood of Malachi's day is set forth in such striking introductory words to verses
8-9, "But you have turned aside from the way." The irony of the
whole situation was that the concern generally was with the
people "turn[ing] aside" from the verdict rendered by the priests
in Deuteronomy 17:11, but now it was the priests who were guilty
of that very deed. Furthermore, they were turning their backs on
the whole "way" of life taught in the Scriptures. The result could
only be tragedy in their own lives and a corrupting influence in
the lives of others. As verse 8 noted, "You have caused many to
stumble by your instruction; you have corrupted the covenant of
Levi."

While there is no formal mention of a "covenant with Levi" in
the Old Testament, Jeremiah 33:20-21 ("If you can break my
covenant with the day and my covenant with the night . . . then
also my covenant with David my servant may be broken . . . and
my covenant with the Levitical priests my ministers.") and Nehemiah 13:29 ("they have defiled the priesthood and the covenant of
the priesthood and of the Levites") presuppose that such a
covenant did exist in earlier times. However, Moses did commis-
sion the tribe of Levi in his final blessing in Deuteronomy 33:8-11
with the responsibility of teaching, offering guidance through the
Urim and Thummim even though it is not called a covenant.
Perhaps the events behind all these allusions to a covenant were

8. See Kaiser, *Old Testament Theology,* pp.85, 120-21.

the same ones that had impressed the psalmist (68:18) and Paul
(Eph. 4:7-10), viz, Numbers 8:5-19 and 18:6-20. In these texts, it is
repeatedly stressed that the Levites were "taken" (8:6, 18:6) and
"given" back to God "from among the people of Israel in place of
the firstborn of all Israel" (8:16, 18:6,8) "to do the service for the
people of Israel at the tent of meeting, and to make atonement for
the people of Israel" (8:19, 18:7). Therefore, since these had been
"gifts" to the Father and their task was to serve on his behalf the
congregation, he was able to return on high after he had descended on Sinai!

That is precisely the apostle Paul's point about the Christian
ministry, for while he recognizes that grace has been given to all
(Eph. 4:7), nevertheless, some men have been *taken* captives and
given as gifts to the Father. Christ, therefore, was enabled to return
to the Father, just as the Father had ascended from Sinai after he
had descended to reveal the Decalogue and to take the Levites
captive. And now these captives carry on the Father's will—some
being apostles, some prophets, some evangelists, and some
pastor-teachers—by equipping the saints for the work of the
ministry until we all come to the unity of the faith.[9]

It was in such a context that God said, "I am your portion and
your inheritance" (Num. 18:20). This seems to be tantamount to a
covenant even though there is no use of that word in this context
or a ceremony such as is given in Genesis 15:12-16. The times had
changed, and Malachi could only shake his head and say, "But
you . . . !" (2:8).

The result of such moral corruption was that the priests
themselves lost all respect in the eyes of the people—as well as
with God! Having courted popularity by modifying God's requirements so as to regard persons and to show partiality in justice
and the proclamation of the message, they were left with egg on
their faces as the community turned away from them. They were
now reaping what they had sown. Is it any wonder that religious
teachers have lost so much face and esteem with today's youth
and public in general? Is it not directly traceable, in most cases, to

9. I am indebted for these observations to my former student, Gary V. Smith, "Paul's
Use of Psalm 68:18 in Ephesians 4:8," *Journal of the Evangelical Theological Society*
18(1975): 181-89.

their failure to live exemplary lives and to faithfully teach God's Word when it is convenient and when it isn't? Neither God nor his Word will be mocked without dreadful consequences.

Love for God's People (2:10-12)

Just as the ancient proverb said "like father, like son," so here one could say "like priest, like people." Water can only rise to the level of its source, so the spiritual level of a people can only be expected to rise to that level attained by its spiritual leaders. Alas, however, Israel's spiritual leaders faltered, and the people did so along with them. This led to an outbreak of problems, including three which Malachi turned to here: disloyalty to the spiritual unity of the national family (2:10), disloyalty to their spiritual families (v. 11-12), and unfaithfulness to their individual family lives (v. 13-16). Included in Malachi's charges were spiritual harlotry, mixed marriages with unbelieving partners, adultery, and divorce! So to the long list of indictments against the priests already announced in Malachi 1:6, there is added this: their failure to teach the truth could now be seen in the devasting collapse of marriage and the family as God had ordained it.

Whether this section (v. 10-12, or 10-16 for that matter) bears a close connection with the preceding section depends on how the question of verse 10 is answered: "Have we not all one father?" It also depends on whether the priests, along with the people, have been guilty of this abusive treatment of their marriages and wives.

Keil would definitely begin a new section here with no connection to the preceding one. He argued, as did Koehler, that "there is no indication in verses 10-16 that the priests gave any impulse through their bad teaching to the breaches of the law which are here condemned; and the violation of the covenant of the fathers and of the marriage covenant forms no more a thought by which the whole is ruled, than the violation of the covenant with Levi in the previous section."[10]

However, the question of Malachi 2:10 would appear to link up

10. Carl Friedrich Keil, referring to Koehler in *The Twelve Minor Prophets,* 2 vols., tr. James Martin (Grand Rapids: Wm. B. Eerdmans Publishing Co., 1954), II, 447.

with 1:6 when we realize that this "father" is not "Abraham your father" (Isa. 51:2) as Jerome and Calvin thought, or Malachi's frequently mentioned patriarch, Jacob (Mal. 1:2; 2:12; 3:6) from whom the twelve-tribe nation descended, but Yahweh as in 1:6 where this long indictment began. God is the father of this nation, and he is the one who "created" Israel (cf. Isa. 43:1, "Thus says the Lord that created you, O Jacob"). Obviously, then, by the "we" and "us" of verse 10 Malachi intends his fellow Jews and is not thinking of the universal brotherhood of man and the fatherhood of God. The connection with the preceding section may also be established by the context of 2:1-9. Do we not have here some of the prime examples as to how these priests "cause many to stumble by [their] instruction"? Are these not the grievous results of the ministry "turn[ing] aside from the way" (2:8)? Does not Malachi intend these sins to be a partial catalogue of what happens when the ministry does not keep God's ways, but shows partiality and avoids certain issues in which society has taken the lead (v. 9)? If the answer to these questions is yes, it would certainly explain why this section begins so abruptly with a question and without a vocative such as verse 1 has.

So a call is issued for a new loyalty and love for the whole people of God, Israel—his body of believers—and we must be reminded of our common origin and rebuked for our disloyalty one to another. God's fatherhood is not related to the whole of creation or to the whole world, but only to his creating the one people of God. The tragedy was that Israel had become so crass as to "say to a tree, 'You are my father'" (Jer. 2:27). And they had also neglected their fraternal ties one to another. Forgetting that what hurt one of them hurt all the body, they began to join themselves in marriage to heathen women or to put away by divorce their own wives in defiance of their obligations to one another, to the body, and to the covenant of marriage to which God was a witness!

Wounding the whole body is not a slight offense in either the Old or the New testaments. In the New Testament there are two passages that are sometimes confused since they seem to say the same thing, but a close inspection of the difference in the singular and plural pronouns will show otherwise. In 1 Corinthians 6:16-20 the text does warn of the individual danger of joining oneself to a prostitute. It askes, "Do you (sing.) not know that your body (sing.) is a temple (sing.) of the Holy Spirit within you, which you have from God? You are not your own; you have been bought with a price. So glorify God in your body." But in 1 Corinthians 3:16-17 the point is different: "Do you (pl.) not know that you (pl.) are God's temple and that God's Spirit dwells in you (pl.)? If any one destroys God's temple, God will destroy him. For God's temple is holy and that temple you (pl.) are." What a stern warning! To be responsible for introducing that which could destroy and disrupt the whole people of God would be to invite a similar divine judgment on our lives for so doing. Who said the community or local body of believers was not all that important; it is only the individual that counts? Neither Malachi nor Paul would stand for such unbiblical thinking or acting. All schismatic elements in my speaking, acting, and thinking toward the one people of God must desist and be repented of, lest a similar fate fall on my own life.

"Why then are we faithless to one another" (Mal. 2:10b). Every form of sin, including marrying foreign women, divorcing the wives of their youth, joining themselves to foreign gods, and more, was an act of treachery against the whole body, the individual family units, and God. Where was the "true instruction," from the Levitical mouth in times like these? How could this people—or even we today—profess to be the bride when they have gone into spiritual adultery—as also often happens in our day? Physical and spiritual adultery are often linked together, and thus God's covenant with his people is profaned. God had called his people by his own name. He had declared them to be "my son, my firstborn" (Exod. 4:22), even his "special possession," a "holy nation," of "royal priests" (Exod. 19:5-6), but look at them now!

God had set Israel apart from the other nations when he made a covenant (Mal. 2:10; cf. also Exod. 19:5-6; 24:8) with their fathers: Abraham, Isaac, and Jacob. But Israel was now desecrating that covenant and acting in a treacherous and treasonous manner toward his brothers by marrying heathen women and divorcing their Israelite wives. The word to "deal treacherously" (v. 10,11) is from the Hebrew verb *bāgad* and is related to *beged*, "garment." In effect then, this was a "cover-up" job; it was a masking of the covenant that God had with his people. Therein lay the treachery!

From this general statement we go to the specific charge of mixed marriages in Malachi 2:11. The issue was not cross-cultural marriages of different races; instead, it was a mixing of religions and spiritual commitments that was being objected to here. The expression "daughter of a foreign god" referred to an idolatress; one who was dependent on that deity. Such marriages were indeed taking place as reported in Ezra 9:2-6; 10:18-19; Nehemiah 10:30; 13:23-27, even though Scripture had forbidden such (Exod. 34:11-16; Deut. 7:3; 1 Kings 11:1-2).

The result was that Israel, whom Yahweh called "holy," the one chosen from all the nations to be his holy people, a royal priesthood, and special possession (Exod. 19:5-6; Deut. 7:6; 14:2), had profaned herself as the sanctuary of God. Ezra will prefer charges against the priests, the Levites of his day, for intermarrying with pagan nations (Ezra 9:1-3). Likewise in Malachi, the long list of sins continues from 1:6. As Paul asks in 2 Corinthians 6:15-16, "What has a believer in common with an unbeliever? . . . What agreement has the temple of God with idols?"

God's response to this violation of his covenant is that such individuals will eventually find their family wiped out, for the Lord will "cut off . . . all such, *root and branch.*" This last idiom is almost impossible to translate. Some suggest "everyone who awakes and answers"; others "teacher and student," or "watcher and respondent." The general intent is clear: the idiom meant that the entirety of the transgressor's family would be involved in the "cut[ting] off."

The fact that Malachi may still be pointing the finger at the Levites is seen in the last clause of verse 12. Since the priests were given the role of presenting the offerings to the Lord (Mal. 1:7; 3:3), Malachi may be warning that there would be no one left to present sacrifices to the Lord. At any rate, no one would be left in the entire family of any guilty man, to worship the living God. They all would be "cut off" from the "tents of Jacob," a phrase that recalled Israel's humble origins in those nomadic days of the patriarchs, but which now functioned to indicate her collective communal heritage in the many dwellings that had come out of the patriarch Jacob. None who loved the people of God could or should act in such a wicked way, for God would take it no lighter than he takes the same action today against his church (1 Cor. 3:16-17).

Love for God's Gift of a Marriage Partner (2:13-16)

Accusations continue: "And this again you do" (Mal. 2:13).[11] The issue of divorce that is to be treated in this section is just as abominable to God as were the religiously mixed marriages condemned in verses 11-12. Long before any of the violators realized or even acknowledged the gravity of their sin, they became aware of some of the results. The Lord refused to recognize their sacrificial gifts and prayers to him because of their sin against their wives. In an effort to get God's attention, these guilty offerers redoubled their efforts to placate God's anger, while carefully avoiding the subject of their sin or displaying any desire to forsake that sin.

Whether the weeping was the heartbreak of the divorced wives which poured forth as a mist that clouded the altar from the sight of the Lord (though women did not ordinarily approach the altar, their tears could be spoken of as a figurative covering of the altar, as the Targum and Jerome infer) or the increased intensity of the guilty worshipers who drenched the altar "with tears, with weeping and groaning because the Lord no longer paid attention to [their] offering or accepted it" is difficult to say. More weight perhaps rests with the second suggestion, even though both are possible interpretations.

Again that conversational style of Malachi is seen in verse 14. The prophet hears the people ask, "Why does he not [pay attention or accept our offerings any longer]?"[12] The answer is, because of the broken marriage vows which were not only made between the two parties, but made with God as a witness! That marriage is viewed as a covenant as can also be seen from

11. Cf., however, Robert Altmann, "Malachy 2, 13-14 and UT 125, 12-13," *Biblica* 58(1977): 418-19. He would render v. 13a "Even indignity, gnashing of teeth you perform, covering with tears Yahweh's altar."

12. Ibid., p.420, argues for two reasons given here: "Because Yahweh was a witness," and "because [ᵃšer] you have deceived her."

Proverbs 2:17 and Ezekiel 16:8. This nuptial contract could not be lightly regarded since it had all the solemnity of an oath and was attended by the very presence of God as one of the witnesses. He it was who would punish any violations of this covenant.

In order to illustrate all the more graphically the aggravation that the offense of divorce worked, Malachi used three phrases: "wife of your youth," "your companion," and "wife of your covenant." The later phrase made it clear that the wife who was divorced was one of the daughters of Israel, this covenant people; hence a sin against her was a sin against God. The tender memories and associations of youth are raised in the other two phrases. Said T. V. Moore,

> She whom you thus wronged was the companion of those earlier and brighter days, when in the bloom of her young beauty she left her father's house and shared your early struggles, and rejoiced in your later success; who walked arm in arm with you along the pilgrimage of life, cheering you in its trials by her gentle ministry; and now, when the bloom of her youth has faded and the friends of her youth have gone, when father and mother whom she left for you are in the grave, then you cruelly cast her off as a worn-out, worthless thing, and insult her holiest affections by putting an idolater and a heathen in her place.[13]

Solomon had enjoined couples, in that profound allegory on marital and conjugal fidelity in Proverbs 5:15-21, to "rejoice in the wife of your youth" (v. 18). Perhaps there is an echo of the "one flesh" of Genesis 2:24 in the word "companion," which means "united, or joined together." "It implies harmony, a desire to work together to achieve life's greatest goals while sharing all the hardship, the pain, and the joy."[14]

The last two verses of this section present some difficulties of their own, but especially verse 15. It is rightfully labled a *crux interpretum*. Many interpret the "one" as referring to Abraham making *'eḥād*, "one," a nominative. "Did not one [viz; Abraham] do so?" i.e., take a pagan Egyptian named Hagar as his wife? The

13. T. V. Moore, *Haggai, Zechariah, and Malachi: A New Translation with Notes* (New York: Robert Carter & Bros., 1856), pp. 362-63.

14. Wolf, *Haggai and Malachi*, p 92.

prophet would then be viewed as conceding the point and replying yes; but it was for the purpose of raising up a "godly offspring."

But this interpretation is open to a number of objections. Abraham is never called by the name "the one," nor could his conduct in "putting away" Hagar be considered to be the case being discussed here, for the wives who were being divorced were covenant wives and not pagan wives. Furthermore, Abraham did not divorce Sarah when he took Hagar as his wife; Hagar was brought into the picture because of Sarah's wishes, not in disregard for the wishes of the wife of his youth as was true in Malachi's day. And what shall this view make of the Hebrew, "and the remnant [or 'residue,' $\check{s}^e{}'\bar{a}r$] of spirit was his [or 'belonged to him']"? It is too mild a rendering to suggest that it means "to him, i.e., to Abraham, was a remnant of intelligence" (F.J.V. Maurer). Finally, in every case in Malachi where the people raise an objection (as this view claims they have done in v. 15), that objection is introduced by the formula, "You say" (Mal. 1:- 2,6,7,12,13; 2:17; 3:7,8,13). Therefore for these reasons we cannot make Abraham the "one" mentioned in this text.

Since the subject under discussion is divorce, what would appear more typical of this Hebrew prophet than to return to the originating passage where the marriage ties had been set forth with the same degree of solemnity as argued here? It would be as conclusive an argument as our Lord will later make in a similar situation where divorce is also the subject, "Have you not read, that he who made them from the beginning made them male and female, and said, 'For this reason a man shall leave his father and mother and be joined to his wife, and the two shall become one flesh'? So they are no longer two but one flesh" (Matt. 19:4-6; cf. Mark 10:7-8).

The subject then would be God and "the one" would be the object and equal to the "one flesh" of Genesis 2:24. Even though there is no explicit indication in the first clause that it is an interrogative or that the "he" is God, both possibilities are accepted here as being consistent with the context and Hebrew grammar and syntax. The thought would then run like this: Why did God make Adam and Eve only one flesh, when he might have given Adam many wives, for God certainly had more than enough of the Spirit, or his creative power, in reserve to furnish many partners? However, our God was seeking a godly offspring, and such plurality would not have been conducive to this result. This solution seems to be the more preferable one.

Another class of interpreters makes the subject "the one God" and asks "Has not one God created us?" "And did the one God create them? And what did the one God seek?" But why this stress on the oneness of God in a text where the oneness of marriage is at stake?

The same could be said about yet another interpretation that translated *lo' 'ehād*, "no one" or "not one" and made it a simple affirmation instead of a question. It also supplied from the previous sentence the object of "made" and the predicate of "the one" in the second clause. The result was something like this: "Not one, or no one who has any spiritual insight, has ever done anything like *this* to his wife!" However, the position of *w^elo'*, "and not," and the question in the second clause make it almost certain that a question and not an affirmation is intended here in the beginning of verse 15. Moreover, the prophet would have had to say *'ēn 'īš* (cf. Gen. 39:11) or simply *'ēn*, had he meant to say "no one." Finally, this interpretation uses *'ehād* to refer to different subjects; the first to "no one" and the second "one" to Abraham ("And what about the one?" or "And what did the one [i.e., father Abraham] do?") even though this second "one" has the article with it and would naturally refer back to the former.[15]

One other major option has been suggested by Patrick Fairbairn and T. V. Moore.[16] This view advocated that "the one" refers to the "one chosen seed," i.e., the nation of Israel. Moore suggested that since the prophet had argued that the Jewish people had one father in verse 10, these mixed marriages to pagans had violated this oneness. Did not God make us one nation by separating us from the other nations? asks this view. Yet this limiting was not done because the Spirit of God had exhausted the fullness of his blessings, which might have been spread more widely among other nations, but it was done specifically so that he might make

---

15. The critique of this interpretation follows Packard, *Malachi Expounded*, p. 17.

16. Moore, *Haggai, Zechariah, and Malachi*, pp. 365-66; Patrick Fairbairn, *The Christian Treasury* (Edinburgh: Johnson, Hunter & Co. 1847), p. 187.

from the "seed" a repository of his covenant and the stock of his Messiah. The introduction of idolatry, polytheism, and related sins into the one people of God broke this unity and would lead, unfortunately, to the amalgamation of the chosen people into the families of the earth. However, this view, while offering several attractive features, does not appear to be as consistent and forceful as the one that refers it to the "one flesh." The sin reproved, it must also be noticed, is more than idolatry or polytheism; it must address the problem of divorce and this view fails to go beyond the recognition of Israel's holy calling as a nation and the introduction of wives from noncovenantal backgrounds or faith. Yet this passage leads into the fact that these men have been unfaithful to their wives in that they have divorced them.

This close connection between Malachi 2:15 and what follows can now be seen in the introductory word in verse 16, "for" or "because." The subject of the verb, "I hate" is the Lord God of Israel. This change from the third person to the first person is not all that uncommon.

Scripture here records one of its strongest protests against divorce, the putting away of wives. In no uncertain terms, God is represented as loathing the practice and the results. This verse, however, must not be viewed as a direct contradiction to Deuteronomy 24:1 where divorce is not approved but is given some strictures of written notice and is attributed to the hardness of men's hearts rather than a change in the divine attitude to the practice (see Matt. 19:3-8). The Deuteronomic law was given not only to supply the woman with written protection against wife-swapping or uncertainty about her true marital status, but it was especially meant to prohibit the remarriage of these two partners after one or the other had been married to someone else.

God's hatred is further expressed in these words; "one who covers his garment with violence." The traditional rendering, "who covers violence with his garment," is grammatically impossible since 'al with the verb must designate the thing covered, not the covering itself (cf. Num. 16:33; Deut. 13:8; Ps. 106:15; Hab. 2:14).[17]

The word "garment," no doubt, refers to the ancient custom of

17. See Moore, *Haggai, Zechariah, and Malachi,* p. 367 for this observation.

spreading a garment over a woman, as Boaz did over Ruth, to claim her as a wife (Ruth 3:9; cf. also Deut. 22:30; Ezek. 16:8) and designated the conjugal relation by metonymy even as "bed" functions in our day. T. V. Moore cites a parallel Arabic expression in which "to cover the garment with violence, was to act in a violent and unjust manner toward the conjugal relation, just as to be unfaithful to the bed is to be unfaithful to the nuptial obligations."[18] Thus what was meant as a symbol of wedded trust became the agent of violence toward these wives.

This section concludes with a warning, "So take heed to your spirit and do not be faithless." This is a repetition of the warning given in verse 15c.

Accordingly, each of these four affections signals a call to the priesthood (as well as to the laity) for a whole new quality of life. With deft accuracy and penetrating incisiveness, the illness of the people of God and the society of that day were laid at the feet of an anemic ministry that chose to trifle first with God's glory, then his Word and his congregation, and finally with their marital relationships. Could it be that the word Paul gave in 1 Timothy 4:16 was stimulated by the repeated warning of our text, especially verses 15c and 16c? Paul exhorted Timothy: "Take heed to yourself and to your teaching; hold to that, for by so doing you will save both yourself and your hearers." A complete and total love for the living God will evidence itself in seeking first the glory of God. It will exhaust every ounce of energy to teach only what is true and faithful from the Word. It will enjoy God's people and seek to build them up, and it will make every effort to preserve faithfully that covenant made with the wife of one's youth to which God was a witness.

18. Ibid.

4

A Call to Trust an Unchanging God
(Malachi 2:17–3:12)

Sometimes the circumstances of life can be so harsh and so contrary to expectations that the ungodly are led to an outright denial of the providence of God in the affairs of men and women. Such a challenge to divine providence was made by the distraught Jews of Malachi's day. To their way of thinking, the prosperity of the nation and its people was long overdue! The preaching of Haggai and Zechariah (around 520 B.C.), now a century past, had not resulted in any dramatic reversal of fortunes—at least as far as Malachi's generation was concerned.

The cause of such a state of affairs, however, was clear. The people had purposely neglected the more important commands of God but had meticulously set out to fulfill the less significant duties to God, hoping thereby to obligate God to prosper them. Instead of inferring that their privilege as a chosen nation brought greater obligation and consequently higher guilt and punishment, they pointed to a few token evidences of their religiosity as grounds for their complaint of being treated unfairly by God. "Why," they protested, "should evil-doers, like the neighboring heathen, be so prosperous and so free of divine punishment?" Their monstrous conclusion was this: either God loved and rewarded evil-doers; or if not, Where was the God of justice? One thing or the other had to be true; either there was no directing hand of God in the affairs of men or God favored the wicked.

The identity of these bitter logicians in Malachi 2:17 becomes clearer in 3:7, 13-15. They were those who "turned aside from [God's] statutes" and harshly concluded that "the arrogant" were "blessed," for there was no "profit" to be realized in keeping God's command or in serving him. In fact, they are contrasted with "those who feared the Lord" (3:16). Accordingly we cannot classify those who wearied God either as pious Israelites who for the moment were overwhelmed by the pressures of their day or as middle-of-the-roaders (somewhere between outright pagans and holy believers) whose faith was emerging but was not yet deep enough to handle the difficulties of real life. Neither group will match the strong words of Malachi.

The words of these complainers belong to the mocker and scorner. Their words put a constraint on God, and they reversed the truth as God had revealed it. This is not to say that there are no occasions when the righteous cry out in doubt over the prosperity of the wicked and the apparent unfairness of life. Such moments of questioning appear in the lives of both Jeremiah (12:1) and Habakkuk (1:2-4). In fact, Asaph said, in his famous Psalm 73, that his feet had almost slipped over the edge of propriety on this question of the prosperity of the wicked—until he "entered the sanctuary of God" and considered "their final destiny" (Ps. 73:17; cf. also Pss. 37 and 49).

Surprisingly, these cynical unbelievers did long for the coming of the Messiah. However, they had an incorrect view of the purpose and the result of Messiah's coming. It was their hope that all the injustices and poverty they had suffered would now be instantaneously rectified—to the discomfort of all the surrounding Gentiles.

Thus, it was not skepticism or doubt over the ultimate coming of Messiah that Malachi needed to address in chapter 3, but delusions about the purpose, effects, and results of Messiah's coming. God would not change one iota from his present nature or method of working.

Messiah would come, as these mockers had expected. But he would come suddenly, and he would come without the results falsely attributed to him.

The heart of our text, therefore, contains the focal point and subject for our message: "I the LORD do not change" (Mal. 3:6). This is the doctrine of the immutability or the unchangeableness of the living God. While all else may change in this age of "future shock" (Alvin Toffler's phrase), the nature, attributes, qualities, being, and person of God may be counted on as a fixed point of reference and as one in whom there is no variableness. Such unchangeableness, of course, must not be confused with frozen immobility—as if God were stuck with some blind force or law to which he was bound no matter how much he might wish otherwise to benefit his children. God can change in his actions toward us as much as any other living person can change. What he cannot and will not change, however, is the consistency of his own person as the basis on which these decisions are made. That is the comforting feature of his unchangeableness.

Two of those *qualities* (our homiletical keyword) may now be traced in Malachi 2:17-3:12. The outline for our passage is:

1. Our God is just—the issue at stake—2:17–3:6
    A. In his preparation—3:1a
    B. In his coming—3:1b-2
    C. In his refining—3:3-4
    D. In his judgment—3:5
    E. In his long-suffering—3:6
2. Our God is faithful—3:7-12
    A. In his call—3:7
    B. In his challenge—3:8-10
    C. In his promise—3:11-12

We find two main paragraphs in this section of thirteen verses beginning with Malachi 2:17. This is another example of a very poor chapter division since most of what we now call chapter 3 is intended in answer to the charges of 2:17. Thus the answer to the question, "Where is the God of justice?" is found immediately in the theme sentence of 3:1, "Behold, I will send my messenger to prepare the way before me."

The theme of the second paragraph is, "Return to me, and I will return to you, says the LORD of hosts" (3:7). This, in turn, leads to a whole discussion about how individuals may return—and ultimately—to a trust in the faithfulness of the God who promises to "pour down for you an overflowing blessing" (v. 10).

But behind these exaltings of both the justice and faithfulness of God is that pivotal claim of the whole passage: "I the LORD do not change" (Mal. 3:6)—neither in my justice nor my faithfulness; not in the present or in the future!

Our God Is Just (2:17-3:6)

With a strong figure of speech, Malachi allows that the cynics have succeeded in wearying God with their constant complaints about his partiality to the wicked and to pagans like the Persians. Now while it is true that "the everlasting God . . . does not faint or grow weary" (Isa. 40:28) from the demands of his office, work, or the plethora of the needs of mankind; we may speak in the fashion of men (an anthropomorphism) and say that Israel's sin (and ours) did indeed weary God and his patience (Isa. 1:14; 43:24).[1]

And so the question-and-answer style opened another new subject and section in this book just as Malachi 1:2 and 1:6 had functioned previously.

Using the same innocent naiveté as previously, Malachi's audience found it hard to believe that they (!) had made God weary with their words. How was this possible?

Malachi located it in two assertions and one question:

1. Everyone who does evil is good in God's eyes.
2. He takes pleasure in them.
3. Besides, where is the God of justice?

The structure of both assertions lays emphasis on "everyone doing evil" and "them." Like little children caught in the act of doing wrong and who instinctively point to the other children and ask, "What about them?" so these arrogant complainers pointed to everyone else and asked, "What about them?"

The charges, of course, were as monstrous as they were wrong. To justify either the wicked or their wickedness was "an abomination to the LORD" (Prov. 17:15) and calling "evil good and good

1. Wolf, *Haggai and Malachi*, p. 97. Also see Ralph H. Alexander, "*Yāgēa'*," *TWOT*, I;360.

evil" was enough to call down one of Isaiah's indictments of "woe" (Isa. 5:20).

To say, therefore, that God esteemed evil-doers as good and actually took pleasure in them was nothing short of blasphemy. The word "to delight, to take pleasure in," Hebrew ḥāpēṣ, is properly used of God as when he "delights" in his law being kept (Isa. 56:4); in "mercy," "knowledge of God" (Hos. 6:6); in "justice," "covenant love," and "humility" (Mic. 6:8); or in "truth" (Ps. 51:8). But the scoffers of Malachi's day reversed all this. As far as they were concerned, since Yahweh had not favored them with material prosperity, his influence and favor must be going to the wicked Persians and not to the chosen people of Israel.

With more than a tinge of sarcasm, the people summarized their complaint with the question: "Where is the God of justice?" That quality of God which had so long served as the theme of Israel's prophets was in short supply. But that only raised the point—"justice"? According to what standard? From the prophetic view, the standard was supplied by the very character of God. For the prophet's contemporaries, it was measured chiefly by their own material prosperity—that is, what was fair, just, and good. Yet unwittingly they were, under the circumstances, asking God to reveal his judgment, for the same Hebrew word can be rendered "justice" or "judgment" (as in Mal. 3:5). Unable to see the hand of God in the movements of their time or to discern the rebuke of God in their present situation, they longed for the arrival of the God of justice. But they clearly mistook the purposes of that coming for exactly the same reason that they doubted the providence of God in the affairs of their present lives.

Nevertheless, their question would be answered—even if it was not the answer they had expected. They would learn that God was indeed just and this justice would be observed in five different ways:

In his preparation (3:1a)

That long-expected day of Yahweh was about to dawn, but it would not be the panacea for all the ills of life that so many unprepared people had imagined. In fact, Amos sternly warned his eighth century B.C. audience not to long for the day of the Lord unless they were thoroughly prepared for the arrival of Messiah

(5:18); otherwise, the results would be as terrifying as those of a man who escaped a near-tragic confrontation with a lion and a bear only finally to be bitten by a snake!

"Where is the God of justice?" The Lord God himself answered this query. "Behold, I send my messenger to prepare the way before me" (Mal. 3:1a). Obviously this announcement was received and founded in Isaiah 40:3-5: "A voice cries: 'In the wilderness prepare the way for the LORD; make straight in the desert a highway for our God'."

The situation was a familiar one in the ancient Orient, for whenever a king was about to arrive at a town or village, messengers were sent ahead in order to allow the towns and villages to make the necessary preparations to receive their royal guest. Likewise, God would be announced by a promised forerunner.

This messenger (mal'āk) was not an angel, a spiritual being, or even the one often called the "angel [or messenger] of the Lord" in the Old Testament. He was an earthly mortal who will explicitly be connected with the prophet Elijah (Mal. 4:5, Hebrew text, 3:23) who will herald the arrival of the second advent of Messiah.

In the meantime, however, that announcing voice is equated with John the Baptist in the Lord's first advent and incarnation. This is not a case of double-talk, double meanings, or equivocation.[2] For if we are able to receive it, Jesus explained, John the Baptist was that Elijah who is to come (Matt. 11:14) because he came in "the spirit and the power of Elijah" (Luke 1:17). Again in Matthew 11:10 (=Luke 7:27) he clearly stated, "This (autos) is he of whom it is written, 'Behold I send my messenger before thy face, who shall prepare the way before thee'."

However, John was just as clear that he was not Elijah: "I am not [Elijah]" (egō ouk eimi, John 1:21,23). John, no doubt, denied that he was Elijah according to the popular misconceptions entertained by the people of the day. Nor was he the final or real Elijah who would announce the second advent. Thus, the scribes expected Elijah to come before Messiah arrived, and indeed he had come (elthōn, past tense) and he was in the act of "restoring

2. For further details on this problem, see Walter C. Kaiser, Jr., "The Promise of the Arrival of Elijah in Malachi and the Gospels," Grace Theological Journal 3(1982): 221-33.

(*apokathistanei*, present tense) all things" (Mark 9:12). Matthew, in referring to the scene on the Mount of Transfiguration as Mark had done in the verse quoted above, combined the present with the future tense: "Elijah does come (*erchetai*, present tense), and he is to restore (*apokatastasei*, future tense) all things" (Matt. 17:11). The restoration to which Jesus was referring is no doubt the same one mentioned in Acts 3:21—a future work connected with the *parousia* or second coming of our Lord.

The preparatory work of this messenger was that of "clearing the way before [the Lord]." It meant leveling the road, filling in the ruts, removing the boulders and straightening its course (Isa. 40:3; 57:14; 62:10) for the arrival of earthly monarchs. But when applied to the Lord of glory, it had a moral and spiritual preparation in mind. The figure of speech was merely transferred from one realm to the other. The idiom was also used of "clearing the ground" for the planting of the vine, in this case Israel (Ps. 80:9), or of "clearing up" a house for Abraham's visitor (Gen. 24:31).[3] Once again, the evidence points to a spiritual housecleaning as the only proper preparation for the arrival of Messiah.

In his coming (3:1b–2)

The Lord's answer to the scorner's question could be put in one Aramaic word: *Maranatha*, i.e., "the LORD comes" (1 Cor. 16:22). For now that the messenger had prepared the way, the Lord (Hebrew, *'ādôn*)[4] would come back suddenly.

The God of justice whom men sought (2:17; 3:1) is here variously identified with the "Lord" (*'ādôn*), "the angel (or 'messenger') of the covenant" (*mal'ak habb'rît*) and owner of the temple (*hêkālô*). Since the word "Lord" is singular and has the article (*hā'ādôn*), it is certain he is God since *'ādôn* with the article always has this meaning (Exod. 23:17; 34:23; Isa. 1:24; 3:1; 10:16, 33, etc.).[5] *'ādôn* also is the title borne by Messiah in Psalm 110:1. It signifies ownership; he is owner and master of everything.

The fact that God himself is the speaker and has just declared

3. This connection is pointed out by Wolf, *Haggai and Malachi*, p. 98.

4. Baldwin, *Haggai, Zechariah, Malachi*, p. 242, n. 1 points out "that *'ādôn* is interchangeable with Yahweh is proven by such verses as Zechariah 4:14; 6:15, *'ādôn* of the whole earth'."

5. Moore, *Haggai, Zechariah, and Malachi*, p. 376.

that the way is to be prepared "before *me*" does not detract from this identification of "the Lord," for he simply equates "me" with "the Lord" and "the messenger of the covenant." Here, as in Psalm 2:2-3, the speaking God is at one and the same time uniquely One, and yet he has One who proceeds from him who is called "the Lord" or "the messenger of the covenant" (not to be confused with "my messenger," the announcer). Surely this statement is tantamount to a recognition of the second person of the Trinity.

It is clear that this One who is sent from the Father is the One Almighty God with supreme authority, for (1) he is owner of the temple: "He will come to *his* temple." (2) He is also called "the Lord" whom men were seeking: the God of justice of Malachi 2:17. (3) He also was equated with "me" in the Father's speech for whom the way was being cleared. Thus, the Father announced, "Behold *I* am sending my messenger who will prepare the way before *me* and *he* will come suddenly to *his* temple, even the Lord whom you are seeking." This easy, sudden, but important transition from first person "me" to "he" is extremely significant for a proper understanding of this passage.

At first, we are tempted to equate "*he* will come" of verse 1 with the announcing messenger ("my messenger," *mal'akî*). But that option is quickly removed as we learn in rapid order that this can be no mere mortal or angelic being. He is "the Lord," the owner of the temple, one with the speaking God, the God whom men are seeking, even the messenger of the covenant whom men profess to take such delight in.

What does this last title mean: "Angel (or 'messenger') of the covenant"? Which "covenant" does he mean? The Mosaic covenant? The covenant made with Levi (Mal. 2:4-5)? The new covenant Jeremiah had heralded? And which "messenger" or "angel" does he intend?

When Malachi's prophecy is read against the background of the informing theology[6] of the Scriptures in the hands of the Jewish community at that time, it will be clear that the covenant and its contents were a unity even though there was a plurality of forms and times in which the covenant was given. Thus the

6. Walter C. Kaiser, Jr., *Toward an Exegetical Theology*, (Grand Rapids: Baker Book House, 1981), chap. 6.

single plan of God was the one promise-plan contained in a long succession of covenants beginning with Eve (Gen. 3:15), Shem (Gen. 9:27), Abraham (Gen. 12:1-3), continuing on with Moses (Exod. 6:2-8), David (2 Sam. 7:12-19) and concluding with the *renewal* of that covenant for the new age to come in Jeremiah 31:31-34.

The angel of this promise-plan was the same One whom God had sent ahead of Israel in the exodus from Egypt to guard their way (Exod. 23:20-23; cf. Judg. 2:1-2). We must make no mistake about the identity of this angel, for God's "name is in him" (Exod. 23:21; *š^emî b^eqirbô*). To equate the "name" of God (which stood for his person, his attributes, his character; in short, himself) with this angel was to call him God. Nevertheless, while he was one with God, he also was "sent" from God. Therein lies the essence of the mystery of the Trinity (cf. John 10:30,36). This same "messenger" or "angel" (*mal'ak*) is elsewhere called the "Angel of the Lord." He is the one who appeared in human form to Abraham, Hagar, Jacob, Joshua, Gideon, and Manoah and is variously called the "angel of God" (Judg. 13:6,9), "angel of his face (or 'presence')" (Isa. 63:9; cf. Exod. 33:14,15) or more frequently, the "angel of Yahweh" (Gen. 16:9-11; Judg. 6:12; 13:3, etc.). Since he is always treated with the marks of deity, as he is in Malachi 3:1, this "Angel of the Lord" is to be identified with the preincarnate Christ. Both in his person and his functions, he is God—but he also is sent from God (as Exod. 23:20 makes clear).

The New Testament continues to strengthen this equation already made in the Old Testament. Christ is the mediator of the old and new covenants—now called the new (or better still—based on the large amount of continuity in its provisions—the *renewed* covenant); (Heb. 8:8-13). The "mediator of the new covenant" (Heb. 12:24) was the same Christ or Messiah who originally made this covenant with his people when he bought them up out of the land of Egypt (Judg. 2:1-2; cf. Exod. 23:21-22). He is our Lord and Savior as well.

Thus, there are three persons, not just one or even two in verse one. There is (1) the speaking Father, (2) the announcing prophet ("my messenger"), and (3) the sent Lord or messenger of the covenant. And it is clear that the Sent One is just as fully God as the Father who speaks in verse 1, for he is "the Lord," the owner of

the temple of God, and one who conveyed the covenant contain-
ing his everlasting plan of the promise to mankind throughout all
the ages.[7]

His coming would be "sudden" (pit'ōm), i.e., unexpectedly
rather than immediately. This word appears twenty-five times in
the Old Testament and in every case except one (2 Chron. 29:36) it
is connected with disaster or judgment.[8] Accordingly, for the
wicked the coming of the Lord would be "as a thief in the night" (2
Pet. 3:10; note in that context as well the scoffers were also asking
where was the coming promised).

His coming would signal the beginning of judgment, but not
the judgment that the scoffers of Malachi 2:17 were hoping
for. Instead the "day of his coming" was that "day of the LORD"
so frequently mentioned in the prophets (Joel 2:11; Amos 5:18,
and others).

That day is the time when God would visit them in judgment for
their own sins. Exodus 32:34 was the first to herald: "In the day
when I visit, I will visit [or punish] their sin upon them." For
unprepared people, that day would be a dreadful event. It would
be "darkness, and not light" (Amos 5:20), a day of wrath, trouble,
and distress, a day of ruin and desolation (Zeph. 1:15). "The day of
the LORD is great and very terrible; and who," asks Joel, "can
endure [or bear] it?" (Joel 2:11). Malachi 4:5 will call it "that great
and dreadful day of the LORD."

Instead of enjoying the destruction of the Gentile nations and
restoring prosperity to these sarcastic seekers who professed to
"delight" in the arrival of God, that day would be a nightmare of
trouble before which no unbeliever could endure, much less
stand and hold ground in the presence of this dreaded judge. It is
a strong delusion to desire and long for the return of Christ in
order to bring those temporal blessings we have not yet enjoyed.
That day is only a day of salvation, joy, and deliverance for those
who truly believe in Messiah. And that day is to be located in a
period yet future, even as the New Testament also teaches by
alluding to this same text in Luke 21:34,36; Ephesians 6:13; and

---

7. See the development of this thesis, part 2 in Walter C. Kaiser, Jr., *Toward an Old
Testament Theology* (Grand Rapids,: Zondervan, 1978).

8. Victor P. Hamilton, "pit'ōm," *TWOT*, II, 744.

Revelation 6:16-17. Thus we are to be watchful, vigilant, and in prayer that we may escape all these judgments. The only provision for standing in that day is the whole armor of God (Eph. 6:13) or in terms of Psalm 24:3-4, "clean hands and a pure heart."

In his refining (3:3-4)

The cleansing work of God is depicted in two figures; fire and soap. What fire does in separating the slag from the metal and soap does in separating dirt from clothes, so will the cleansing work of God do for his people. Thus the judgment of God held no threat for his people, just as the real metal had nothing to fear in the fire or the clothes had to dread of the laundryman's soap or lye. But pity the slag and dirt. They would risk everything—and so were the unbelieving scoffers in Israel. For them the furnace of affliction would be dreadful. Their garments were covered with violence (Mal. 2:16) and with stains of sin which no ordinary soap or human efforts could remove (Jer. 2:22; 4:14); these same two figures of cleansing had appeared in Isa. 1:25 and Dan. 12:10.

Thus the fire would test every man and his work. Much of what had been accomplished by men and women in their lifetime would be disclosed for what it, in fact, was—wood, hay, and stubble (see 1 Cor. 3:11-15).

This cleansing or refining[9] would begin the same spiritual leadership that had been so instrumental in leading Israel astray, as Malachi charged in chapters 1 and 2; viz, the priest. Whereas charges had been preferred against the priesthood in 1:6–2:9, now the cleansing would start with this group and then extend to the whole nation. God would "purify" (ṭihar) the "sons of Levi," for Levi was the tribe assigned the duties of the temple, and one of its families, the sons of Aaron, were its priests.

---

9. On the emphasis given to silver, see Alan Robinson, "God, The Refiner of Silver," *Catholic Biblical Quarterly* 11(1949): 188-90. Refining silver is a more delicate process. When molten, it gives off twenty times its own volume of oxygen with a hissing and bubbling known as "spitting." "Unless the molten silver is treated with carbon (charcoal was used by the ancients), the silver reabsorbs oxygen from the air and loses its sheen and purity" (p.189). But there is a second reason: "How does the refiner know when the silver is ready? . . . There is a dramatic moment when he knows that all dross has gone from it. Peering over it, the silver suddenly becomes a liquid mirror in which the image of the refiner is reflected. Then he knows that his task is done" (p.190).

As Levi was cleansed, they were enabled to give to the Lord "offerings in righteousness" (Mal. 3:3). Such sacrifices were possible only when both the spiritual condition of the offerer and the quality of the offering were without blemish. Only then will the offerings once again become acceptable and be received by God with favor (v. 4). They would bring pleasure and refreshment to God, whereas wickedness had previously "wearied" both God and men.

But if this refinement of Israel's Levitical and priestly establishment is still future even to our day, must we infer that this text has application to the offering of the Eucharist (i.e., in the Roman Catholic view of the Lord's Supper) or to the reinstitution of the animal sacrifices (perhaps in the millennium)? Neither of these suggestions will work here, for the offering is not the offering of the Righteous One, i.e., Christ (vs. the view of some Roman Catholics), nor can the removal of these sacrifices "once for all" (Heb. 10:10,14,18) be retracted and others added to the completeness of Christ's final sacrifice of himself. We conclude, therefore, that Malachi speaks of offerings in the righteousness, just as he spoke in 1:11 of "pure offerings" in "every place" (NIV), to signify authentic worship of God in the future under the terms and rubrics of worship known in his own day. Just as the prophets describe the final battle on earth in the end time under the rubrics of armament of their own day (e.g., horses, bows, spears), so Malachi describes worship in equivalent terms from his day. We conclude, then, that the *form* of sacrifice may change, but the *essence* and the act of worship remains. It would include the sacrifice of the lips and of praise (Hos. 14:2; Heb. 13:15) and the reasonable service of the living sacrifice of lives dedicated to God (Rom. 12:1-2).

Already in the New Testament we begin to see the firstfruits of such a work among the "sons of Levi," for Acts 6:7 singled out the fact that "a great many of the priests were obedient to the faith" and believed that Jesus was the promised Messiah.

In his judgment (3:5)

The problem with the mockers and their vacuous quibble was that they did not fear God. They, of course, had professed otherwise in 1:6, but their involvement in seven sins was enough to suggest the opposite. While complaining that they, not the pagans, should have been the objects of God's blessing and material prosperity, they proceeded to indulge themselves in all sorts of insolent behavior.

As the Lord introduces his case against the impudent, three legal terms are laid down in rapid fashion in verse 5: "come near" (qārabti), "judgment" (mišpāṭim, the very word they had used in their question of 2:17, "Where is the God of *justice?*"), and "witness" (ēd). God would himself be a "swift witness" when he began to prefer charges against Israel.

Everyone of the seven sins listed was a breaking of God's laws. "Sorcery" or witchcraft was forbidden in Exodus 22:18, Leviticus 20:27, and Deuteronomy 18:14. "Adultery" was forbidden in the Ten Commandments (Exod. 20:14), as was "swearing falsely"[10] (Exod. 20:7; Lev. 19:12). Likewise, oppressing the poor and cheating the laborer out of his daily wages were serious infractions of God's standards of morality (Lev. 19:13; Deut. 24:14-15). Unprotected widows, orphans, or aliens were not to be cannibalized by the vultures of society (Exod. 22:22-24; Lev. 19:10; Deut. 24:19-32; Zech. 7:10).[11] All such sins are causes for the judgment of God. Depriving others of justice in the courts (e.g., "aliens") or taking advantage of a widow or orphan was tantamount to offending God himself. It showed a lack of "fear," i.e., positively, of belief in him and negatively, of regard and respect for the severity of his judgments.

In his long-suffering (3:6)

The focal point of this whole passage has been reached: "I the LORD do not change."[12] Thus the being and character of God

10. The septuagint, 8 codices of de Rossi, 16 of Kennicott, and all extant Talmud mss. add "in my name." See David B. Freedman, "An Unnoted Support for a Variant to the MT of Mal. 3:5, *Journal of Biblical Literature (JBL)* 98(1979): 405-6.

11. See chap. 9 in Walter C. Kaiser, Jr., *Toward Old Testament Ethics* (Grand Rapids: Zondervan, 1983) for a fuller discussion of this last point and earlier chapters in that book for an analysis of the other sins listed.

12. Nahum M. Waldman, "Some Notes on Malachi 3:6; 3:13 and Psalm 42:11," JBL 93(1974): 543-45, on the basis of Akkadian intransitive usage of the parallel word *enû,* "change," would prefer to sharpen the translation to: "For I, the Lord, *have not gone back on my word"* (italics mine).

remains dependable and without any vacillation. Psalm 102:26-27 declares that while all else perishes and wears out, God "remains the same."

Israel owes her continued existence to that same unchanging purpose and character. Had not the Lord been gracious and patient, Israel would never have continued to exist. God had promised that he would never "change" his word of promise to Abraham and David (Ps. 89:34, where the word for *"change"* is the same one used in Mal. 3:6).

How just and fair is our unchangeable God! Even when Israel "violated" or "profaned" the covenant God made with her (Mal. 2:10) God refused to "violate" that same covenant (Ps. 89:34, the same Hebrew word is used in both contexts).[13] Little wonder, then, that our God is celebrated for his justice and judgments even when he was being accused of failing on both points.

Our God Is Faithful (3:7-12)

The consistent nature of our unchanging God can be seen in the second quality or attribute of his nature, i.e., his faithfulness. That quality is evident in the gentle way in which God continued to deal with these hardened sinners. Instead of summarily rejecting them and ceasing to show them any affection, he reviews with Malachi's audience how persistent his love has been. It has continued even though "since the time of your forefathers you have turned away from [my] decrees" (3:7). While Israel has remained fickle and undependable, the living God has never flagged in his decision to choose, bless, and love Israel. That is unchangeableness on an extraordinary level! He has not changed at all.

In his call (3:7)

One of the keywords of the prophets was this word for repentance, i.e., "return" or "turn" [back to the Lord] (*šûb*). In fact, the message of all Israel's prophets could be put in this one word, "return" (Zech. 1:3-4). Once again, that same call was issued. Israel, and all who will ever hear this call, are urged to turn one

---

13. As observed by Wolf, *Haggai and Malachi*, pp. 105-6.

hundred and eighty degrees and to reverse their direction. Instead of heading off toward sin, self, and contemporary idols, Israel is urged (and we with her) to turn around and look in faith to the man of promise.

Thus we learn in this call why the complainers of Malachi 2:17 had waited in vain for any judgment on the nations or for their own prosperity and deliverance. The problem was not to be found in God, but rather in Israel who had continued to rebel against her Lord since the time of her founding fathers, even though they continued to regard themselves as holy and righteous.

Once again, however, Israel failed to acknowledge her problem and instead gave that whimper of innocency by saying in effect, "Who? Us? We need to repent? We need to turn back to God? We never went away. So why do we need to turn anywhere?!"

With such impenitence, how could God "turn" in the blessing the people so desperately craved? The only thing left to do was to embarrass them by pointing to one glaring example of where Israel had refused to turn to the Lord: the area of their tithing to God. This is not to say that it was their only sin or that this sin has a status greater than any other. But it did show that these complainers were willing to cheat God out of what was due to him. They were willing to neglect God's people, to injure the wives with whom they had made a covenant of trust, to neglect or to despise the placing of unblemished offerings on the altar of God, and to defraud God in giving tithes and offerings.

The main verb in Malachi 3:8 occurs only here and in Proverbs 22:23 and is usually translated "to rob, defraud, or overreach" (*qāba'*). Joyce Baldwin observes, however, that the verb is "well established in the Talmudic literature to mean 'to take forcibly'."[14] She went on to note that many moderns by transposing the Hebrew consonants (a process named *metathesis*) give the verb *'āqab*, "to circumvent," "to assail insidiously," a root from which Jacob's name is formed. But there is no need (or textual evidence) to resort to such a revision of the text. Taking what belonged to God was outright thievery and fraud.

God had required the tithes and offerings from time immemorial. Cain and Abel already in Genesis 4 worshiped with gifts

14. Baldwin, *Haggai, Zechariah, Malachi*, pp.245-46.

placed before God. Abraham gave the priest Melchizedek a "tenth" of his booty taken in rescuing Lot (Gen. 14:20). And under the instructions given to Moses, a "tenth" (our word "tithe" in Mal. 3:8, *ma'ăśēr*) was "holy to the LORD" (Lev. 27:30). This was given to the Levites (Num. 18:24). From this tithe, or tenth, the Levites paid a "tenth" to the priests (Num. 18:26-28). Others who benefited from the tithe were those families entertained at the temple (Deut. 12:18), widows, orphans, and resident aliens in their midst (Deut. 14:28-29). The "offerings" (*tĕrŭmâh*) were those portions of the animal sacrifices designated for the priests (Exod. 29:27-28; Lev. 9:22; Num. 5:9) or those gifts that were given voluntarily for some special purpose (Exod. 25:2-7). But all these Israel had, in part or in their entirety, withheld. But whenever revival had broken out in Israel, the joyous giving of the people had started simultaneously (cf. Neh. 10:38ff; 2 Chron. 31:5-19).

In his challenge (3:8-10a)

As a result of such stingy giving—itself an indicator of their spiritual density—a curse rested on Israel and all that they did. They were cursed with crop failure, low yields, and barrenness. Israel was to make no mistake: it was God himself who had been defrauded; not the Levites or the religious institutions of Israel! (The pronoun "me" in v.9 is emphatic, coming first in its clause with the adversative particle attached.) Thus, no one robs God without robbing himself at the same time.

But if they (and we) would wish to see the justice of God once again, then Israel (and we) must start by taking his commands seriously. Malachi 3:10, therefore, issues a new challenge to obey. The "whole nation" (v.9) had been implicated in the curse and, as other prophets had so frequently observed (e.g., Hag. 1:5ff; Zech. 5:1-4), this affected the general productivity of all the land.

The situation, of course, was as old as the fall of man in the garden of Eden. Since man was made of the dust or dirt of the earth, when he sinned the dirt was likewise affected for his sake (Gen. 3:17-19). But when man experiences the final act of God's redemption in the second coming of Christ, the whole of creation, and even the ground, will be released (Rom. 8:19-24).

The "storehouse" (*bêt hā'ôṣār*) is either the "treasury of the temple of the LORD" (1 Kings 7:51) or, in a more figurative sense, the place from which all of God's blessings proceed. The word "treasury" is found eighty times in the Old Testament, but in only a few can it clearly be connected with a divine storehouse (e.g., Pss. 33:7; 135:7; Job 38:22). Deuteronomy 28:12 (and in a lesser way Jer. 50:25) does say God's treasure-house is in the heavens. Accordingly, we must be careful about using this verse to insist on "storehouse tithing" by which some require that *all* giving to God's work must be channeled *only* through the local church! We must indeed "bring" the tithes, but in fairness to the text, the "storehouse" is not equated with the local church.

Malachi also stresses in his challenge from God that this must be "the whole tithe" (*'et kol hamma'ăsēr*). This stress on wholeness must have meant the firstfruits of the crops, their shekels, and offerings; but it also included their time, their talents, and *themselves*. This was always the cry of the prophets. God inspected the giver's life *first*, and then he regarded the gift placed on the altar. "Bring," he challenges, "the whole tithe into the storehouse."

This challenge also included a "test" (*bāḥan*, "to examine, try, prove"). This root and its derivatives appears thirty-two times in the Old Testament and often is found paralleling the verbs "to smelt or refine" (*ṣārap*) and "to put to a test" (*nāsâh*). "*Bāḥan* partakes of both senses in that it denotes examining to determine essential qualities, especially integrity."[15] The key difference is that *bāḥan* usually has God as its subject, and it is used "almost exclusively in the spiritual or religious realm."[16] God is willing to let his people learn for themselves on a firsthand, experience level the truth of his oft-repeated promises.

In his promise (3:10b-12)

In response to the obedience of men's hearts as evidenced by this one area of giving, God will release the "floodgates" or "windows" of heaven and send abundant rains (cf. Deut. 28:12; 2 Kings 7:2,19). In fact, he will send so much that men will not be able to contain them all. This phrase in Malachi 3:10 is literally, "until a failure of sufficiency." This could either mean until we

15. John N. Oswalt, "*Bāḥan*," *TWOT*, I. 230.
16. Bruce K. Waltke, ibid.

lack room to contain all that God sends us or until the heavenly source has been exhausted due to the heavy demand made by so many believers. The same idiom occurs in Psalm 72:5; until a failure of the moon, i.e., as long as the moon endures. So here in Malachi it could mean "as long as the sufficiency of God endures." Regardless of which option is chosen, both are hyperboles for the fact that God dares his people to exhaust and so strain his goodness that he might, as it were, need to withdraw the offer temporarily due to such heavy drain on the resources of heaven! Of course, such a state of affairs is laughable: but God's grace is not and neither is his challenge.

Moreover, God will "rebuke the devourer" (probably, locusts). He will rebuke them by commanding them to halt their destructive progress. But the teaching of verse 11 applies to every impediment that arises to frustrate the labors of men and what they wish to accomplish.

The result of obeying this challenge will be that men everywhere "will call you blessed"—the very promise God had originally given to Abraham in Genesis 12:1-3 and parallels (cf. Ps. 72:17). The land now under the harsh thumb of Persia could be a "delightful land" (Mal. 3:12, NIV). Israel would see once again how faithful this unchanging Lord was.

What a great God! How excellent are all his qualities, but especially these two which are celebrated and expounded in this passage: his justice and his faithfulness. Both attributes are clear indications of the fact that he does not change or alter in his character one iota.

We must therefore stop inferring from the inequality of the human condition that there is some evidence that God is indifferent to the human condition or that he has decided to let up on his standards of right and wrong. Such careless thinking and living will land us in the lap and the camp of those complainers of Malachi 2:17.

We must also do more than merely desire the coming of Christ; many do that for reasons of prosperity, safety, or deliverance. We must await that day with great anticipation—yes. But we must also be in a constant state of preparation, for that day will be a dreadful one for those who are not prepared.

Because God is both a fire for the impenitent and a refiner unto sanctification for the believing, we must say amen to all his works and not fear any of them. Only the dirt and the slag need fear the cleansing and the fire, but real clothes and genuine metal will last and endure any amount of testing.

Finally, we must again realize that we are preserved by the unchangeable character of God. We must never trust our unchangeable love or service of God as the basis on which our hope rests. We indeed are called "to turn" and "repent" of all our sins and offenses against God, but in the end, we will be delivered solely on the basis of his unchanging character, being, and word.

No, God is not indifferent to the wickedness of men and, yes, he will come and come unexpectedly. There is, then, all the more reason to heed his challenge and put him to the test. We will begin by giving him the whole of ourselves, our talents, time, and gifts; and let us see for ourselves that he does love to benefit his children in such grand measure that they will scarcely be able to contain them all.

5

A Call to Take Inventory
(Malachi 3:13–4:6)

The mentality that concludes the church "has had it" does not originate in our day. Malachi found the same pattern of thought. All too frequently contemporary churchgoers act as if God owes them something once they have participated in, or merely attended, services in the house of God—no matter how cold or bankrupt the real affections of their hearts were in that service!

Such a mercenary approach to serving God and attending his house is strong evidence that worldliness was at the root of the problem. Without giving any concern for the spiritual motives or the requirements of true heart confession, the malcontents of Malachi's day demanded the rewards they felt God had owed them. The brashness with which their "charges" ("your words," 2:17; 3:13) were leveled against God are startling, for out of their own lukewarmness, they ordered God to favor them with great rewards.

This is a classic example of inauthentic and unreal worship of God. In such cases it is not the institution of the church that "has had it" or is in trouble, but those who have been playing church. God hates lukewarm worshipers. In Revelation 3:15-17, God threatened the Laodicean churchgoers with rejection because they were neither hot nor cold. He would spit them out of his mouth. And that is the fate of all Pharisaism. It is not, however, the fate of the church or of all true worship of God. That earthly instrument,

95

designated by God for the honor, glory, and service of his name, has only begun to show the real power the Father has invested in it. Neither the Old Testament temple nor the New Testament church had anything to fear from God; but reckless, false, heartless, pretenders had everything to fear from his hand.

Accordingly, our text asks three *questions* (our homiletical keyword) in its call for men and women everywhere in all ages to take inventory of their lives. These questions are:

1. Is it vain to serve the Lord?—3:13-18
2. Is there no difference between the wicked and the righteous?—4:1-3
3. Are there no guides for righteousness?—4:4-6

The first question is introduced by the speech of the arrogant (Mal. 3:14), and it is evaluated against the response of the wicked (vv. 13-15) and of those fearing God (vv. 16-18). Verse 18 provides a transitional thought as we are introduced to the alternative prospects for the one serving God and the one who does not in 4:1-3. Implied is Malachi's question; "Is there no difference between these two groups as these boastful complainers have charged?" Finally, we are introduced, in an abrupt transition, to Moses and Elijah: the one as a commander of the ordinances of God and the other as a restorer of the hearts of men and women before that great and terrible day of the Lord comes. Malachi here offers to answer the question, "What about any guides to lead us back to God and the righteousness you advocate?" These, then, are the issues before us.

Is It Vain to Serve the Lord? (3:13-18)

Two groups are surveyed as an answer to this question is sought: the proud complainers and the believing God-fearers. Their responses could not have been any more opposite to each other.

The proud complainers (3:13-15)

Once again, the skeptics had offended God with their words (Mal. 2:17; 3:13). Their words were strong,[1] impudent, and presumptuous. They were bold and confident to excess.

"'Put me to the test,' says the LORD, and I will bless you" (Mal. 3:10). But these skeptics had replied in effect, "The wicked have tested and proven God already. The wicked sin and God has done nothing about it. We conclude, therefore, that God is a paper tiger. He threatens but he is unwilling or unable to act and do anything about his threats." The prophet continued, "But the nations will call you blessed and happy if you will test him and do what he says." Such a prospect, however, was only greeted with more jeering. With unmitigated insolence the skeptics chorused as if they were presenting diplomas to a graduating class, "We now officially pronounce all the *wicked* the most blessed or happy." The situation was almost beyond repair.

Such impudent speeches as these never passed the lips of some of the most hard-pressed saints of God, e.g., troubled Asaph or hard-hit Job. In their deepest despair they never reached the conclusions of these godless complainers. The impiety of their lives can be found in three offenses: their words, their attitude, and their method.

Taking these offenses in reverse order, it is clear that their method was wrong. They "conversed with one another" (the Hebrew verb is a Niphal form that has a reciprocal meaning of conversing, or even gossiping, one with another, cf. Ezek. 33:30; Ps. 119:23) "against" the Lord (Mal. 3:13). Rather than directing their complaint to God, as Jeremiah, Job, or Asaph had done, they turned their doubts into beliefs, which they shared with their fellow citizens.

Their wrong attitudes can be seen in the description of their words, which were strong or impudent (Mal. 3:13) and in the effect these words had on God ("You have wearied the LORD" 2:17 NIV). Like the priests, they had "despised" God and

---

1. Waldman, in *JBL* 93(1974): 545-48 would translate *hzq 'L* as "Your words *have been too much for me*" (italics mine) based on neo-Assyrian and neo-Babylonian examples.

all that he stood for (1:6) and had "sniffed at" his requirements
(v.13).

With their evil words they made three bold assertions
(Mal. 3:14):

> There is no use (*šāwe'*) *in serving God.*
>
> There is no profit (*beṣa'*) *in observing the commands of God.*
>
> There is no profit in fasting or repenting.

Each charge must be considered separately.

Service ('*ābad*) to God was useless; it was worth nothing. The
word they used is most familiar in the third commandment, "You
shall not take the name of the Lord your God in *vain.*" Thus, its
primary meaning is "emptiness, vanity." It labels all alleged
service to God as unsubstantial, unreal, and without value or
worth, material or moral, to the practitioner.

In addition, they alleged that all observing of his commandments or carrying out of his requirements resulted in no profit to
the worshiper. There was no pay, no increase, no observable
return in material prosperity, political influence, or the like.
To keep his charge was equivalent to carrying out all that
God had said, as Abraham had (Gen. 26:5) or as the minister-
ing priests did in the tabernacle and temple (Lev. 22:9; Num.
3:6-8; 2 Chron. 13:11; Zech. 3:7). Since the Hebrew word "profit"
(occurring thirty-nine times in the Old Testament) was a
technical term for weavers cutting a piece of cloth free from
the loom. Its use in Malachi had the negative connotation
of men expecting their "cut" or percentage, as a racketeer or
gangster would demand his "cut" for his evil work (cf., e.g.,
Gen. 37:26).[2]

The last impudent claim was that there was nothing to be
gained from "walking in mourning before the LORD of hosts" (Mal.
3:14). The word translated "mourning" is usually connected with
the verb *qādar*, "to be dark." The idea is that some had clothed
themselves with dark sackcloth or even blackened their faces to
convey apparent grief and sorrow for the sin and plight of their

---

2. Oswalt, "*Beṣa'*," *TWOT, I; 123.*

nation. But the whole venture was a sham. It attributed worth to the act itself, even though the outward act was as devoid of genuine piety as it was for those in Isaiah's day (Isa. 58:2-12). God always inspects the heart of the one fasting before he regards the fasting itself.

The particle of inference opens Malachi 3:15: "But now" (NIV). These skeptics will now make their most atrocious insinuations. They reverse the affirmation of God in verse 10. They mockingly pronounce that the arrogant are "blessed," the evildoers "prosper," and those who put God to the test "escape." God had promised to bless Abraham if he obeyed, but now, they claim, he is rewarding the wicked with happiness. Furthermore, they assert that the proud are built up, established, and prosperous; an allusion, no doubt, to the midwives whom God blessed by building them into permanent families [="houses"] in Israel (Exod. 1:21; cf. Jer. 12:16-17). These last two charges were introduced by the Hebrew particle *gam*, "and" or "also," which placed the two clauses in parallel or equal footing to each other and to the preceding clause.

The believing God-fearers (3:16-18)

At the same time ("then," 'āz), there was another group that spoke to one another, but the content of their conversation was substantially different. Their words were about the fear of the Lord and the value they place on the name, reputation, and person of the living God. By describing what these believers had done, the prophet in effect told the proud complainers what they ought to have done. He also ceases speaking to his audience in the second person and lapses into the third person as he talks about the believers.

We are told twice that these believers feared the Lord. (Mal. 3:16). It must be a most significant point and an important distinction, for that is where the spiritual leadership of Israel was weakest (1:16), yet God continued to expect respect and reverence of his name (1:11, 2:5; 3:5). Only in a remnant did he find the fear of his person (3:16). The "fear of the LORD" is a virtual synonym for the righteous living or holy lifestyle that grows out of this fear (cf. Lev. 19:14; Deut. 17:19; 2 Kings 17:34). Fear, then, became the motivation that produced holy living and an attitude of complete love, trust, and obedience of the Lord as one's Master and Savior. It was a turning to God in faith for the meaning and enjoyment of life in all its mundaneness and spiritual potential.[3]

But there was a second characteristic of these believers: they "thought on his name" (*hošᵉbî šᵉmô*). In this infrequent usage of a very common verb, the sense is "to meditate," "regard" or "to so focus one's mind" on a thing that one gave great value to that thing (cf. Isa. 33:8; 53:3 for the negative side, "set no value on"; or Ps. 144:3 for the positive, that God should take "account" or "have thoughts" of David). The Septuagint used the same Greek word to translate the Hebrew word in Malachi 3:16 that Paul used in Philippians 4:8, "think on these things," i.e., "take inventory of these things." Therefore, the remnant set their highest value upon the name, i.e., the character and being of the Lord.[4] They made an inventory of that name, and they concluded that it was their wealth, property, and greatest asset. Jesus had said, "Where [our] treasure is, there will [our] heart be also" (Matt. 6:21). Solomon likewise warned, "as a man *thinks* in his heart, so is he" (Prov. 23:7). They thought on the name of God and valued his person as their most prized possession, and this dedication was reflected in their own character.

God, in turn, "listened to" and "heard" the requests of these believers. In fact, their names and actions were written in a book before God. This "book," or more accurately "scroll of remembrance" (*sēper zikkārôn*), should not be confused with the book of life (Ps. 69:28; Rev. 20:12, 15). Here we have something similar to the Persian custom of entering into a book all acts that should be rewarded in the future (e.g., Esther 6:1). But the psalmist knew of such a book: "You have kept count of my tossings; and put my tears in your bottle. Are they not in your book?" (Ps. 56:8; cf. also Dan. 7:10). God had not forgotten what these men and women had endured, nor was he unmindful that

---

3. On the "fear of the Lord/God," see Kaiser, *Toward an Old Testament Theology*, pp. 66-68; 168-71.

4. See Kaiser in *Zondervan Pictorial Encyclopedia*, IV, 363-65

he was the object and center of all their thinking and value systems.

The happiness of these believers goes beyond answers to their prayers or their place in God's book of rememberance. Two promises are added: "They will be mine" and a "treasured possession" in that day when God acts (Mal. 3:17, NIV). What is this but a repetition of the oft-repeated promise that God would adopt the believing remnant of Israel as his own intimate people "with all the rights and privileges pertaining thereto." In Exodus 4:22-23 he called them "my son," "my firstborn,"[5] and in 19:5-6, he adopted Israel as his people.[6] Most surprising of all, Israel was accorded the status of God's "choice or treasured possession" (s^e gûllâh, Mal. 3:17; Exod. 19:5). The basic root of this term means "to set aside a thing or a property." However, unlike real estate, which could not be moved, this property was *movable*. This term is always used in the Old Testament of Israel except for the two references to David's treasures stored up for building the temple (2 Chron. 29:3; Eccles. 2:8). Israel, then, became the object of God's love and affection, and he regarded them as his most prized and treasured personal possession (cf. Deut. 7:6; 14:2; 26:18; and Ps. 135:4; with New Testament applications to the New Testament believer in Eph. 1:14; 2 Thess. 2:14; Titus 2:14 and 1 Pet. 2:9).

When the "day" comes, which God has fixed for carrying out his final acts of judgment and salvation, this believing remnant will be remembered and cared for. God will "spare" them the punishment that will fall on the ungodly. Then men will observe for themselves the difference between the righteous and the wicked; between the one who has served God and the one who has not (v. 18; cf. Ps. 1:1, 4-6; Dan. 12:2). Thus those who assaulted heaven with verbal abuse about how unjust God was in dealing with the presence of evil would "again see" (Mal. 3:18a, NIV) that there was indeed a difference (2:17). In so saying, the prophet has sounded his theme note (1:2), viz., Yahweh's love for Israel.

5. Kaiser, *Toward an Old Testament Theology*, pp. 101-2.
6. *Ibid.*, pp. 103-7.

Is There No Difference Between the Wicked and the Righteous? (4:1-3)

Many Hebrew manuscripts, the Septuagint and the Vulgate along with most English versions, either begin a new chapter or leave an abnormally long space between 3:18 and 3:19. But the best Hebrew manuscripts rightly continue chapter 3 to the end of the book, and so it contains twenty-four verses instead of our eighteen. Indeed, these verses merely elaborate on the theme announced in 3:18.

The prophecy deals with "the day of his coming." That day will be mentioned four times in the closing verses, 3:17; 4:1, 3, 5. And that day is described in ways most reminiscent of Joel 2:11, 31 and Zephaniah 1:14.

In fact, for each of five Old Testament prophets working in four separate centuries, that day was "near" and "at hand" (Ninth century—Obad. 15; Joel 1:15; 2:1; Eighth century—Isa. 13:6; Seventh century—Zeph. 1:7, 14; and Sixth century—Ezek. 30:3). Each of these prophets also saw immediate events of his own generation as very much a part of that same "day of the Lord"; for example, the destruction of Edom (Obadiah), a disastrous locust plague (Joel), or the pending destruction of Jerusalem in 586 B.C. (Isaiah). Nevertheless, that day was likewise a future, but final, day wherein the Lord would "destroy the whole earth" (Isa. 13:5) and reign as king over all the earth (Zech. 14:1, 8-9).

This presents a three-way puzzle: that day is viewed as *one* day that is a *collective* event embracing a number of distinct happenings occurring *successively* in history. But if we were to limit the meaning of that day to any one of these events, it would appear to be exaggerated and unfulfilled since no one occurrence, until the final one in the succession, exhausts the meaning. The prophecy must be viewed as being successively fulfilled through a number of events in history, all of which depict, now one and now another, aspect of that final and climactic fulfillment.

Such a statement of successive fulfillment does not violate the ordinary laws of language or the principle of the single meaning of the text as judged by the truth and the intention of the author/writer. Said T. V. Moore,

Every language contains these formulas, which refer not to any one event, but a series of events, all embodying the same principle, or resulting from the same cause. . . .

We find repeated instances of this species of prediction in the Scriptures. The promise in regard to the "seed of the woman," (Gen. 3:15) refers to no one event, but runs along the whole stream of history, and includes every successive conquest of the religion of Christ. . . .

[This] class of predictions . . . is . . . what the old theologians called the *novissima*.[7]

In like manner, the "day of Yahweh" is a generic or collective event that gathers together all the antecedent historical episodes manifesting the judgment and salvation of God as they pointed to that future grand finale for the whole series. Thus every evidence of God's intervention in history, either to save or to judge men or nations, became a preview, a sample, a downpayment, and earnest money on that climactic conclusion to history.

Perhaps the best way to describe this phenomena is to call it a "generic prediction," which Willis J. Beecher defined as

one which regards an event as occurring in a series of parts, separated by intervals, and expresses itself in language that may apply indifferently to the nearest part, or to the remoter parts, or to the whole—in other words, a prediction which, in applying to the whole of a complex event, also applies to some of its parts.[8]

What would this day, spread over successive centuries with a finale so awesome as to alarm even the unperturbed, reveal by way of distinguishing between the proud and the righteous? The

7. Moore, *Haggai, Zechariah, and Malachi*, pp. 397-98. His sample formulas in English are Berkeley's celebrated line, "Westward the course of empire takes its way" (which "is fulfilled in every new advance of occidental greatness") or the expression "The schoolmaster is abroad" (which "has it fulfillment in every successive teacher of youth who goes forth to his work").

8. Willis J. Beecher, *The Prophets and the Promise* (New York: Thomas Y. Crowell, 1905, reprint Baker Book House, [1970]), p. 130.

destinies of each of these groups in that day was set forth in Malachi 4:1-3.

The destiny of the proud and wicked (4:1)

Once again "behold" is used to capture our attention for an important point. The Lord would return one day and take action against all the wicked. In his anger against their wickedness, that day would be one of consuming fire (a common theme in the prophets: Joel 2:3, 10; Isa. 10:16; 30:27; Zeph. 1:18; 3:8; Jer. 21:14; Ezek. 21:1-4). His anger would burn (Isa. 13:9) as he came "in flaming fire" (2 Thess. 1:7).

As a result all the wicked, the proud, and every evil-doer would be ignited like so much dry stubble or chaff (Obad. 18; Isa. 5:24; Zeph. 1:18). Many cannot believe their eyes when they read a passage like this. Instead they urge that all will be saved—universally. Such universalism incorrectly pits the attribute of the love of God against his justice. Thus they falsely claim that there will be no day of judgment except in the indefinite sense that everyday we reap the bad effects of our bad deeds. They place heavy emphasis on those aspects of the day being realized in this present age (e.g., Acts 2:17) as an excuse for eviscerating all future predictions of judgment from these prophecies. But they fail to deal adequately with the principle of "generic" or "successive fulfillment." As T. V. Moore reminded:

> It is true that the deluge, the destruction of Sodom, Babylon, and Jerusalem, and all the subsequent visitations of God's wrath, were days of the Lord, and in each one of them the proud and evil-doers were as chaff. But as each one did not exhaust these ominous predictions, so all together have not yet met the full reach of the terrors, which will only be done in that future day in which the Lord shall descend from heaven with a shout, with the voice of an archangel and the trump of God, and the drama of earth shall be ended. All previous judgments were but reddenings of the dawn, that betokened the coming, but did not unfold the terrible brightness of that awful day. . . . The finality of this day is distinctly declared in the utter ruin that it is predicted to bring.[9]

9. Moore, *Haggai, Zechariah, and Malachi.* pp. 398-99.

So the wicked finally will be set ablaze in the "furnace" or "oven" of God's anger (cf. Ps. 21:9). How unhappy it will be for those whom the mockers had pronounced happy in Malachi 3:15. It will be totally effective, leaving "neither root nor branch" (v. 1).

The figures of the dread and extent of the terror must not be taken for a literal statement of *annihilation* of the wicked, for God is faithful and he will preserve alive *forever* all whom he has created. But the horrible fact about the fires of God is not located either in the temperature (Fahrenheit or Celsius) or the geography of Hell. We owe more to Dante, Vergil, and Milton than we do to the Bible for these exaggerations. The disagreeable part of this judgment is that it is permanent and everlasting banishment "from the presence of the Lord" (2 Thess. 1:6-9). It will be eternal existence in a place where neither God nor the influence of his Holy Spirit exists—that is impure Hell in all its fury. It is a place where everyone simultaneously does what he wishes to do. This is not freedom, but nightmarish anarchy.

The destiny of the righteous (4:2-3)

For the righteous, there will be the "sun of righteousness." He is that "light of men," the "light of the world," and the "light to the Gentiles." In Jeremiah 23:5-6, he was called "the LORD our righteousness." While some have doubted that Christ is intended by the "sun of righteousness," the context in Malachi 3:1 had led us to expect the righteousness and justice the proud sought (for their own reasons) in the "messenger of the covenant" whom the Father would "send." This view was perpetuated in the Jewish community by the priest Zecharias who blended Malachi 4:2 and Isaiah 9:2 in the messianic situation of Luke 1:76-79. Zecharias, the father of John the Baptist, uses the Septuagint translation of Malachi, *anatelei*, the "sunrise."[10] It would also appear that the Hebrew verb, "to sprout, or spring forth," hence the messianic title "branch" may have also been simultaneously encompassed in this same Greek word.[11]

Thus righteousness in all its consequences and effects (not as

10. Wolf, *Haggai and Malachi*, p. 120.
11. Walter C. Kaiser, Jr., "*Semah*," *TWOT*, II; 768.

justification or forgiveness of sins)[12] will arise for those who fear
the name of God. It will be a time of victory, vindication, and
healing. The reference to "healing" is no doubt "deliverance from
destruction" as in Psalm 107:20. As the sun sends forth its rays
(depicted in many ancient Near Eastern monuments as a winged
sun disc), the long winter of suffering for the righteous will end
with the refreshing, invigorating, and delivering appearance of the
Son of God.

The righteous will "go forth" skipping like calves released after
being penned up all winter long, for the "breaker" has come (Mic.
2:13). But the wicked will be trodden under foot even as Genesis
3:15 and Romans 16:20 had promised. Where Isaiah 63:1-6 pictures
Christ as treading the winepress in that day, this Malachi text
includes all believers aiding in this banishment of all evil and
unrighteousness once and for all (cf. Rom. 16:20). The dramatic
final outcome of history finally will vindicate God's eternal order.

Are There No Guides for Righteousness?
(4:4-6)

Though connection with the preceding context is difficult, it
would appear that Malachi wanted to remind the righteous once
again that the triumph depicted in 4:2-3 was possible only if they
"remember[ed] the law of my servant Moses."

Yes, there is the law of Moses (4:4)

This was no call to formalism or to ritualistic legalism. Instead,
as E. W. Hengstenberg observed,

> The law is referred to here, . . . not according to its accidental and
> temporary *form*, but according to its essential character, as expres-
> sive of the holiness of God, just as [it is] in Matt. v. [5:]17. In this light,
> it is eternally the same in the eyes of God and no jot or tittle of it
> can pass away[13]

It is this point of view that also supplies the connection between
the adjoining verses, both before and after. The coming judgment

---

12. So Keil, *The Twelve Minor Prophets*, II; 468.
13. Hengstenberg, *Christology of the Old Testament*, IV; 190.

is traced to its source, and the source shows how a nation, or an individual can successfully avoid that judgment.[14] Thus God's people and God's law are inseparable. "If the law is not fulfilled *in* the nation, it must be executed *upon* the nation."[15]

Other prophets had attributed the law (at least in the main) to Moses (Isa. 63:11-12; Jer. 15:1; Dan. 9:11, 13; Mic. 6:4), and this postexilic prophet (who should know better if the liberal documentarians have been anywhere near correct) also, in a matter-of-fact way, links the name of Moses with the law and sets Sinai as the place of its disclosure! Malachi was closer to the scene than we are, therefore, it would be well to trust him.

New Testament believers must also be careful not to erect a giant wall of partition between the law and the promises of God, for Paul asked whether the promises of God had, as a matter of fact, abolished the law. (Rom. 3:31). Paul sprang back with a resounding negative; instead, faith had "established" the law of God.[16] Let us be careful not to pronounce more than three-fourths of God's revelation in the Bible obsolescent.

Yes, there are my Elijahs, the prophets (4:5-6)

In keeping with the characteristics of generic, or successive fulfilment, of prophecy, Malachi closes with a promise that God would send that messenger introduced in 3:1 as the forerunner of Messiah. However, he does not say that he will be Elijah the Tishbite,[17] but "Elijah the prophet" and he thereby opens the door for a succession of announcers all the way up to the second advent of Messiah when the first and last Elijah would step forth as the beginning and the end of the prophets.

There is, no doubt, a relationship between 3:1 and 4:5, as can be seen in the repetition in both contexts of

1. "behold"
2. the participle "I am sending"

14. Ibid.
15. Ibid.
16. See an extended discussion of this issue in Kaiser, *Toward Old Testament Ethics*, final chapter.
17. The Septuagint does contain this reading, however.

3. the mission to clear the way and to restore (as found in verbs that imply a "turning")
4. the sending, followed by references to that great and dreadful day of the Lord[18]

Elijah has been selected since he was at the *head* of the prophetic order—all other prophets followed him. He also was a *reformer* whom God raised up in "a remarkably corrupt age, and whose rejection was followed by a particularly terrible day of the Lord, viz. first the calamities inflicted by the Syrians, and then the captivity of Israel."[19]

But Elijah's *spirit* and *power* were passed on to his successor, Elisha (2 Kings 2:15), just as the spirit of Moses came to rest on the seventy elders. Thus, John the Baptist came in that same line of reformers, prophets, and forerunners of Messiah, for he too came "in the spirit and the power of Elijah" (Luke 1:17). And from Elijah's day to ours, a long line of forthtellers have stood in that succession; men like Augustine, Calvin, Meno Simons, Luther, Zwingli, Moody, and Graham.

This is not to say that Elijah himself will not return just before the final coming of Messiah. If Elijah's coming is only to be in his "spirit and power," then what need was there for him to ascend bodily into heaven (2 Kings 2:11)? But even as the scribes believed, Elijah must come once again before Messiah can return (Mark 9:12). Only then can the restoration of all things occur (Matt. 17:11). That "restoration" will include the reestablishment of Israel in her land (Jer. 15:19; 16:15; 23:8; 24:6; Hos. 11:10) and the "establishing of all that God spoke by the mouth of his holy prophets" (Acts 3:21). The return of Elijah, or a new Elijah, as one of two witnesses is described in detail in Revelation 11:3-12. True, he is not named as Elijah, but he is said to "have power to shut up the sky so that it will not rain during the time they are prophesying" (11:6), a clear allusion to Elijah's most famous work.

Malachi 4:5 identifies "Elijah" with the long line of prophets from the day of the Tishbite until now, which consummates in

18. I am indebted to Wolf, *Haggai and Malachi*, p. 123, for this list.
19. Hengstenberg, *Christology of the Old Testament*, IV: 193.

that final new Elijah who precedes the day of Christ. This text concludes by describing their mission: their job is to close the generation gap by turning the *hearts* of fathers and *hearts* of their sons to the Lord. Only as parents and their children individually and together turn to the Lord will there come a healing of the generation gap with parents being reconciled to each other and to their children.

Humanity worldwide must turn to the Lord, or God must come and smite the earth with a "curse" (*ḥērem*). At this, some will nod their heads and expostulate this teacher saying, "I told you so. The Old Testament is not for the Christian church. Look how it ends in Malachi. The last word in our English canon is 'curse,' while the New Testament ends with a 'blessing'."

But this is all too simplistic. The word used here is an extremely delicate word, and it is not the ordinary word for "curse." It is the opposite concept of a voluntary dedication of one's own life, substance, and talents (cf. Rom. 12:1-2). *Ḥērem* is an *in*voluntary dedication of a country, its substance, and its citizens after decades and centuries of resisting the longsuffering grace of God. Finally he must come and forcefully take what truly belongs to him and what no one ever offered to give to him. Jericho was one such *ḥērem*. Thus, if we and our generation and nations will be Canaan in heart, we will also become Canaan in fate even as Leviticus 26, Deuteronomy 28 and Jeremiah 18:7-10 warned.

We conclude then by asking, has it indeed been worthless to serve the Lord? Has God been a paper tiger and rather ineffective in coping with evil in this present age? Is there really no difference between good and evil, righteousness and wickedness, truth and error? Has not the sun of righteousness already come once, and will he not yet come once more? What, when all is said and done, matters the most and possesses the greatest value for us?

The most valuable of all our possessions should be God's holy name. We ought to speak to one another about him, conscious that we speak under his gaze and love. For we, the people of God, are his greatest treasure, and his movable property. There is much to pause over in the seriousness and horror of that coming day of the Lord. Let us ask God to help us to be among those who will fear the Lord and think of and highly value his name.

Suggested Outline and Worksheet for a Syntactical-Theological Analysis

Reading someone else's commentary or series of sermons is one thing; personally producing worthwhile Bible studies, Sunday school lessons, or sermons is another matter altogether. Therefore, in order to make this study on Malachi more transferable and useful for individuals teaching and preaching in the ministries of Christ's church, we have briefly sketched how we went about organizing our study in hope that others will be able to trace our steps when they go to teach the book of Malachi. Furthermore, the same procedures can apply to any book of the Bible.

Our desire has been to supply the reader with a demonstration and application of the principles advocated in *Toward an Exegetical Theology.*[1] This volume would then become, for many, a supplementary volume to the textbook on principles of exegesis (usually called "exegetical theology" in the older curriculum of most seminaries and graduate faculties of theology).

Rather than laying down those principles again, we will merely follow the outline of part 2 of *Toward an Exegetical Theology.*[2] The examples all come from the Book of Malachi. The outline and

1. Walter C. Kaiser, Jr. *Toward an Exegetical Theology* (Grand Rapids: Baker Book House, 1981).
2. Ibid., pp. 69-181. In addition, chaps. 9 and 10 on preaching or teaching from prophetic and narrative passages should be consulted—pp. 185-210.

procedure, however, are exactly what each student of Scripture should strive to imitate when preparing for a Bible study group, a talk at a para-church gathering, a college or seminary exegesis paper, a Sunday school lesson, or a sermon. Obviously, many will wish to make modifications to fit their own style and emphasis; yet, our argument is that without the following components, the chance of that preparation falling stillborn on the ears of its hearers is extremely high.

The process advocated in *Toward an Exegetical Theology* involves five basic analyses or steps in preparing a text for teaching, personal application, or preaching.

1. contextual analysis
2. syntactical analysis
3. verbal analysis
4. theological analysis
5. homiletical analysis

In order to give some definite form to what would otherwise be an almost overwhelming and intractable task, we advocate that the student of Scripture devote seven or eight pages in a large looseleaf notebook with unlined paper for each Biblical passage selected.[3] These pages and the resulting outline may be arranged as follows:

Contextual Analysis (page 1)

Canonical context

The student has probably somewhere along the line completed his or her own study on the overall theme and unifying message of the Bible. One needs to know what the whole forest is about if one is to accurately deal with the individual trees. Consequently, a working knowledge of the historical development of that overall

---

3. Ibid., p. 153. Note the advice that, where possible, a teaching passage normally be limited to six to eight verses in didactic types of Biblical literature; but when working with narrative texts it is necessary sometimes to extend consideration to twenty or thirty verses in order to treat the whole pericope.

theme in each of the epochs of revelation is necessary for the teaching and preaching to have rootage and depth.

Such information may be secured from those Old Testament or New Testament Biblical theologies that trace the development of theology according to a historical grid. In the Old Testament, one could recommend *Toward an Old Testament Theology*[4] and *God's Design: A Focus on Old Testament Theology*.[5]

Record this overall theme at the top of page 1 of your notebook in this manner:

Contextual Analysis

A. Canonical Context: The Promise-Plan of God for Israel and All Others Who Believe

Book and section context

There are two questions here: (1) What is the overall purpose and plan of the book? and (2) What are the natural breaks in the text that form each of the sections?

The overall purpose and plan of the book:

"I have loved you, says the Lord"—Malachi 1:2

"I the Lord do not change"—Malachi 3:6

or "Malachi: God's unchanging love to us."

The divisions of the book we found were usually associated with the format of a prophetic assertion followed by an incredulous denial by the book's first recipients.

To give this a more graphic representation, we advocate using a chart on page 1 which would look something as in figure 2 (be sure to place a summarizing word or two for each section).

Immediate context

Identify in a short paragraph or two what has preceded and what follows the passage selected. If it has a historical or geographi-

4. Walter C. Kaiser, Jr., *Toward an Old Testament Theology* (Grand Rapids: Zondervan, 1978).
5. Elmer A. Martens, *God's Design: A Focus on Old Testament Theology* (Grand Rapids: Baker Book House, 1981).

Figure 2
Malachi

God's love for Israel	Rebuke to the priests	Rebuke for marrying unbelievers and for divorce	Answer to search for God's justice and faithfulness	Destiny of the wicked and righteous
1:1–5	1:6–14	2:1–16	2:17–3:12	3:13–4:6

cal setting (as Mal. 1:1-5 with its reference to Edom), then a heavy use of atlases,[6] Bible encyclopedias and dictionaries,[7] archeological journals,[8] archaeological encyclopedias,[9] and histories of Israel[10] are strongly encouraged. But if the setting is logical, didactic, or theological, then the lines of thought will need to be traced as clearly as possible.

Syntactical Analysis (pages 2-3)

Literary type

Malachi has very little poetry or wisdom literary form in its text. It is mainly, if not exclusively, *prose in the form of a disputation.* While it encroaches on eschatology, it merely verges on the apocalyptic literary form using only a limited number of stereotype phrases such as "the day is coming" or the picture of the torment of the wicked.

Paragraphing

Now that we know the type of literature we are dealing with and the number of sections in the book that carry out its basic

6. E.g., Yohanan Aharoni and Michael Avi-Yonah, *The Macmillan Bible Atlas* (New York: Macmillan Co., 1968).

7. Merrill C. Tenney and Steve Barabas, *The Zondervan Pictoral Encyclopedia of the Bible,* 5 vols. (Grand Rapids: Zondervan, 1975); or J. D. Douglas, *The New Bible Dictionary* (London: Inter-Varsity, 1962).

8. E.g., *Biblical Archaeology Review* or *The Biblical Archaeologist.*

9. Michael Avi-Yonah, *Encyclopedia of Archaeological Excavations in the Holy Land,* 4 vols., (Englewood Cliffs, N.J.: Prentice-Hall, 1975–78).

10. E.g., John Bright, *A History of Israel,* 3rd ed. (Philadelphia: The Westminster Press, 1981).

plan or purpose, it will be necessary for us to go through the book (or in larger books of the Bible, the section we have chosen for teaching or preaching extending for one quarter of a year) defining and delimiting the paragraphs.

It is best to consult four or five versions of the Bible with paragraph markings, independently making our own judgments on where the division should come. Remember, a paragraph (or in poetry, a strophe) is the framework for expressing and developing a single idea. We recommend the grid, shown in Figure 3, for ease in reviewing the whole book.

Topic sentence and syntactical layout

Having made the decisions on the paragraphs, the next step is to identify the theme proposition or topic sentence for each. This sentence may come at the beginning, middle, or end of the paragraph; position, however, will make little difference. A theme may be implied and not stated, in which case the one understood may need to be supplied in a provisional way.

The best way to think through the question of the theme or topic of each paragraph is to do a syntactical diagram (see *Toward an Exegetical Theology*). Take a blank sheet of paper and draw an inch-and-a-half margin on the left side (if we are going to do the analysis in English or Greek) or on the right side of the paper (if we are going to do the analysis in Hebrew or Aramaic). This margin will be used later for placing the teaching/preaching outline alongside of the syntactical outline to see if it agrees and can be validated by the actual expressions and levels of subordination (or indentation) in the diagram.

Each paragraph must be analyzed in its turn for the *grammatical (not* logical) relationship of every sentence, clause, or phrase. Accordingly, everytime a punctuation mark (a comma, semicolon, colon, period, question mark, etc.) appears, we must make a decision and ask, "Which way did the action go?" It is like a traffic intersection: Do we go straight or turn right or left?

Each clause, phrase, and sentence must then be related to the theme sentence *in the order that they appear in the text* with only the simplest form of the theme or topic sentence (stripped of its

Figure 3
The Versions' Paragraphing of Malachi
Literary Format: Prose and a Disputational Sub-type

		AV	RSV	LB	NASB	NAB	NEB	NIV	my own
Chap. 1	1								
	2		2		2	2	2	2	
	3								
	4								4
	5								5
	6	6	6		6	6	6	6	6
	7								
	8								8
	9								
	10								10
	11								
	12	12							
	13								13
	14								
Chap. 2	1	1	1		1	1	1	1	1
	2								
	3								
	4								4
	5								
	6								
	7								
	8								
	9								
	10		10		10	10	10	10	10
	11	11							
	12								
	13		13				13		13
	14	14							
	15								
	16								
	17	17	17		17	17	17	17	17
Chap. 3	1	1	1		1	1			
	2		2						
	3								
	4								
	5		5						
	6		6				6	6	
	7	7			7				7
	8	8							
	9								
	10								
	11								
	12								
	13	13	13		13		13		13
	14								
	15								
	16	16	16		16		16		
	17								
	18								
Chap. 4	1	1	1		1		1		1
	2	2							
	3								
	4	4	4		4		4		4
	5	5	5				5		
	6								

LB column: The Living Bible breaks at every speaker—impossible to determine *thought* paragraphing.

NAB column: Interestingly, the NAB does not make a 4th chapter division, but continues numbering verses as if in chapter 3.

NIV column: Main thought divisions indicated by subtitles.

modifying phrases or compounded objects) written up against the line dividing off the margin set aside for the teaching/ preaching outline. The rest of the sentences, clauses, and phrases will be indented and related to word(s) that they *grammatically* modify with an arrow pointing *down* if the word they *grammatically* relate to follows, or with the arrow pointing *up* if the antecedent came first in the text.

In order to facilitate a wider use of this text and its method, we will provide a syntactical analysis in both English and Hebrew on facing pages for easy comparison or for use by both laity and pastors. Of course, it is better if the student or pastor has the facility of the original language, but the method works almost as well in English if supporting tools are used for the ambiguous situations.

For further description of this method and for eight other examples in Greek and Hebrew (with facing English pages) refer to *Toward an Exegetical Theology*, pp. 95-104, 165-81.

The syntactical analysis for our five messages in Malachi are as follows:

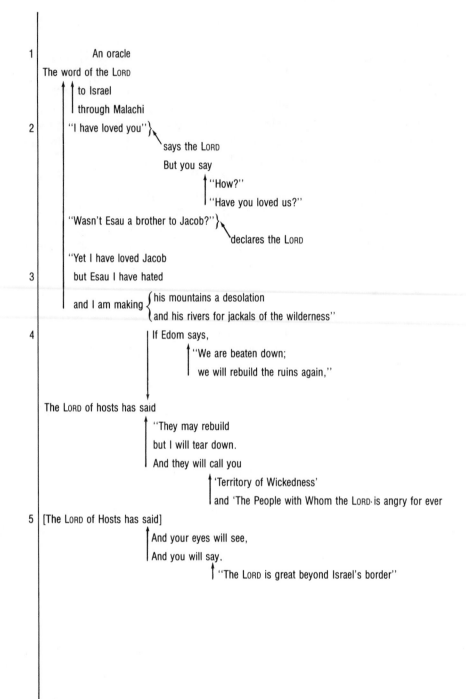

1. An oracle

The word of the LORD

    to Israel

    through Malachi

2. "I have loved you"⎰

    says the LORD

    But you say

      "How?"

      "Have you loved us?"

"Wasn't Esau a brother to Jacob?"⎱

    declares the LORD

"Yet I have loved Jacob

3. but Esau I have hated

and I am making ⎰ his mountains a desolation
           ⎱ and his rivers for jackals of the wilderness"

4. If Edom says,

    "We are beaten down;

    we will rebuild the ruins again,"

The LORD of hosts has said

    "They may rebuild

    but I will tear down.

    And they will call you

      'Territory of Wickedness'

      and 'The People with Whom the LORD is angry for ever

5. [The LORD of Hosts has said]

    And your eyes will see,

    And you will say,

      "The LORD is great beyond Israel's border"

Hebrew text is from *Biblia Hebraica Stuttgartensia* edited by Karl Elliger and Wilhelm Rudolph (Stuttgart: Deutsche Bibelstiftung, 1977). English translation used from Mal. 1:1–4:6 is this author's own translation.

מַלְאָכִי

¹ מַשָּׂא

דְּבַר־יְהוָה

אֶל־יִשְׂרָאֵל

בְּיַד מַלְאָכִי:

² אָהַבְתִּי אֶתְכֶם

אָמַר יְהוָה

וַאֲמַרְתֶּם

בַּמָּה אֲהַבְתָּנוּ

הֲלוֹא־אָח עֵשָׂו לְיַעֲקֹב

נְאֻם־יְהוָה

וָאֹהַב אֶת־יַעֲקֹב:

³ וְאֶת־עֵשָׂו שָׂנֵאתִי

וָאָשִׂים אֶת־הָרָיו שְׁמָמָה

וְאֶת־נַחֲלָתוֹ לְתַנּוֹת מִדְבָּר:

⁴ כִּי־תֹאמַר אֱדוֹם

רֻשַּׁשְׁנוּ

וְנָשׁוּב

וְנִבְנֶה חֳרָבוֹת

כֹּה אָמַר יְהוָה צְבָאוֹת

הֵמָּה יִבְנוּ

וַאֲנִי אֶהֱרוֹס

וְקָרְאוּ לָהֶם

גְּבוּל רִשְׁעָה

וְהָעָם אֲשֶׁר־זָעַם יְהוָה עַד־עוֹלָם:

⁵ כֹּה אָמַר יְהוָה צְבָאוֹת

וְעֵינֵיכֶם תִּרְאֶינָה

וְאַתֶּם תֹּאמְרוּ

יִגְדַּל יְהוָה מֵעַל לִגְבוּל יִשְׂרָאֵל:

A Call to Respond to God's Love

Reasons:

1 I. Because of our God's Election-Love (1:1–3)

2

3

4 II. Because of our God's Justice-Love (1:4)

5 III. Because of our God's Universal Love (1:5)

6   A son honors his father
            and a servant his Lord

           If I am a father

Where is my honor?

          If I am lord

Where is my respect? (fear)

               Says the Lord of hosts

             To you O priests

          (   ) who despise my name

Yet you say

       How's that?

       We have despised *your* name?

7   by placing defiled meat on my altar

Yet you say

       How's that?

       How have we defiled you?

By thinking that the Lord's table is contemptible

8   When you sacrifice blind animals

Is that not wrong? (evil)

     When you sacrifice lame and diseased animals

Is that not wrong? (evil)

    Try offering that to your governor

Would he be pleased with you?

Would he accept you? Says the Lord of hosts

9   But implore now God to be gracious to us

        with such offerings from your hands

Will he accept such on your account?

6 בֵּן יְכַבֵּד אָב וְעֶבֶד אֲדֹנָיו וְאִם־אָב אָנִי אַיֵּה כְבוֹדִי וְאִם־אֲדוֹנִים אָנִי אַיֵּה מוֹרָאִי אָמַר ׀ יְהוָה צְבָאוֹת לָכֶם הַכֹּהֲנִים בּוֹזֵי שְׁמִי ( ) וַאֲמַרְתֶּם בַּמֶּה בָזִינוּ אֶת־שְׁמֶךָ׃	6 	**A Call to Be Credible** *areas*—keyword I. In our profession v. 6–7
7 מַגִּישִׁים עַל־מִזְבְּחִי לֶחֶם מְגֹאָל וַאֲמַרְתֶּם בַּמֶּה גֵאַלְנוּךָ בֶּאֱמָרְכֶם שֻׁלְחַן יְהוָה נִבְזֶה הוּא׃	7	
8 וְכִי־תַגִּשׁוּן עִוֵּר לִזְבֹּחַ אֵין רָע וְכִי תַגִּישׁוּ פִּסֵּחַ וְחֹלֶה אֵין רָע הַקְרִיבֵהוּ נָא לְפֶחָתֶךָ הֲיִרְצְךָ אוֹ הֲיִשָּׂא פָנֶיךָ אָמַר יְהוָה צְבָאוֹת׃	8	II. In our gifts v. 8–9
9 וְעַתָּה חַלּוּ־נָא פְנֵי־אֵל וִיחָנֵּנוּ מִיֶּדְכֶם הָיְתָה זֹּאת הֲיִשָּׂא מִכֶּם פָּנִים אָמַר יְהוָה צְבָאוֹת׃	9	

10 | Oh that someone would shut up the temple doors
That they would not light the fire on my altars in vain
I am not pleased with you—says the Lord of hosts
Therefore I will accept no offering from your hands

11 | Indeed
From the rising of the sun
unto the setting of it
My name will be great
among the nations
and in every place { incense
and
pure offering
They will be brought to my name says the Lord of hosts
because my name will be great
among the nations
—says the Lord of hosts

12 | But you profane it by saying
The table of the Lord is defiled
And its meat, it is contemptible

13 | And you say
What a weariness!
And you sniff at it—says the Lord of Hosts
And you bring
injured
crippled
or diseased animals
And offer them as sacrifices
Should I accept them from your hands? says the Lord

14 | cursed is the swindler
who has in his flock a male
and he vows it
but then sacrifices a blemished animal to
to the LORD
–for I am a Great King—says the Lord of hosts
–and my name is feared among the nations

מִי גַם־בָּכֶם֙ וְיִסְגֹּ֣ר דְּלָתַ֔יִם ¹⁰ | 10 III. In our service
v.10–12

וְלֹא־תָאִ֥ירוּ מִזְבְּחִ֖י חִנָּ֑ם |

אֵֽין־לִ֨י חֵ֜פֶץ בָּכֶ֗ם |

אָמַר֙ יְהוָ֣ה צְבָא֔וֹת |

וּמִנְחָ֖ה לֹֽא־אֶרְצֶ֥ה מִיֶּדְכֶֽם : | 11

כִּ֣י ¹¹ |

מִמִּזְרַח־שֶׁ֜מֶשׁ |

וְעַד־מְבוֹא֗וֹ |

גָּד֤וֹל שְׁמִי֙ |

בַּגּוֹיִ֔ם |

וּבְכָל־מָק֗וֹם |

מֻקְטָ֥ר { מֻגָּ֥שׁ לִשְׁמִ֖י

וּמִנְחָ֣ה טְהוֹרָ֑ה |

כִּֽי־גָד֤וֹל שְׁמִי֙ |

בַּגּוֹיִ֔ם |

אָמַ֖ר יְהוָ֥ה צְבָאֽוֹת : |

וְאַתֶּ֖ם מְחַלְּלִ֣ים אוֹת֑וֹ ¹² | 12

בֶּאֱמָרְכֶ֗ם |

שֻׁלְחַ֤ן אֲדֹנָי֙ מְגֹאָ֣ל ה֔וּא |

וְנִיב֖וֹ נִבְזֶ֥ה אָכְלֽוֹ : |

וַאֲמַרְתֶּם֙ ¹³ | 13 IV. In our time
v. 13–14

הִנֵּ֣ה מַתְּלָאָ֗ה |

וְהִפַּחְתֶּ֥ם אוֹת֛וֹ |

אָמַר֙ יְהוָ֣ה צְבָא֔וֹת |

גָּז֗וּל { וַהֲבֵאתֶ֤ם וְאֶת־הַפִּסֵּ֙חַ֙ וְאֶת־הַ֣חוֹלֶ֔ה

וַהֲבֵאתֶ֖ם אֶת־הַמִּנְחָ֑ה |

הַאֶרְצֶ֨ה אוֹתָ֤הּ מִיֶּדְכֶם֙ |

אָמַ֖ר יְהוָֽה : |

וְאָר֣וּר נוֹכֵ֗ל ¹⁴ | 14

וְיֵ֤שׁ בְּעֶדְרוֹ֙ זָכָ֔ר |

וְנֹדֵ֕ר |

וְזֹבֵ֥חַ מָשְׁחָ֖ת לַֽאדֹנָ֑י |

כִּ֣י מֶ֤לֶךְ גָּדוֹל֙ אָ֔נִי |

אָמַר֙ יְהוָ֣ה צְבָא֔וֹת |

וּשְׁמִ֖י נוֹרָ֥א |

בַּגּוֹיִֽם : |

1   ↓ And now
this is the commandment
               ↑ to you
               O priests.

2   If you will not listen
                   and if you will not take to heart
                        ↑ to give honor
                        ↑ to my name
                            says the LORD of hosts
             then I will send among you the curse
           and I will curse your prosperity.

3   Indeed, I have cursed it
                      ↑ because you have not taken it to heart.
                  I rebuke your seed
                  and I will spread dung upon your faces,
                      ↑ the dung of your festival sacrifices
                  and someone will carry you away to it.

4   Then you will know
                ↑ that I have sent you this command
                   ↑ so that my covenant with Levi may continue
                       ↑ says the LORD of hosts.

5 (My covenant with him has been { life
                           { and peace
 (and I gave them to him
        and he feared me
        and he was awed at my name.

6   Truthful teaching was in his mouth
           and injustice was not found in his speech.
           He walked with me
               ↑ in peace
              and uprightness
           and he caused many to turn from wickedness.

7   ↑ For the lips of a priest should preserve knowledge
              and they should seek instruction from his mouth
                 ↑ because his is the messenger of the LORD of hosts.

8   But you have turned from the way.
       You have caused many to stumble by your teaching.
       You have violated the covenant of Levi
                ↑ says the LORD of hosts.

9   And so I have made you { contemptible
                        { and humiliated
                  ↑ before all the people
              because you { do not observe my way
                      { and show partiality in your instruction

וְעַתָּ֗ה ¹	**1** I. Love for God's Glory
אֲלֵיכֶ֛ם	
הַמִּצְוָ֥ה הַזֹּ֖את	
הַכֹּהֲנִֽים׃	
אִם־לֹ֤א תִשְׁמְעוּ֙ ²	**2**
וְאִם־לֹא֩ תָשִׂ֨ימוּ עַל־לֵ֜ב	
לָתֵ֣ת כָּב֗וֹד	
לִשְׁמִ֔י	
אָמַר֙ יְהוָ֣ה צְבָא֔וֹת	
וְשִׁלַּחְתִּ֤י בָכֶם֙ אֶת־הַמְּאֵרָ֔ה	
וְאָרוֹתִ֖י אֶת־בִּרְכֽוֹתֵיכֶ֑ם	
וְגַ֥ם אָרוֹתִ֖יהָ	**3**
כִּ֥י אֵינְכֶ֖ם שָׂמִ֥ים עַל־לֵֽב׃	
הִנְנִ֨י ³	
גֹעֵ֤ר לָכֶם֙ אֶת־הַזֶּ֔רַע	
וְזֵרִ֤יתִי פֶ֙רֶשׁ֙ עַל־פְּנֵיכֶ֔ם	
פֶּ֖רֶשׁ חַגֵּיכֶ֑ם	
וְנָשָׂ֥א אֶתְכֶ֖ם אֵלָֽיו׃	
וִֽידַעְתֶּ֕ם ⁴	**4**
כִּ֚י שִׁלַּ֣חְתִּי אֲלֵיכֶ֔ם	
אֵ֖ת הַמִּצְוָ֣ה הַזֹּ֑את	
לִֽהְי֤וֹת בְּרִיתִי֙ אֶת־לֵוִ֔י	
אָמַ֖ר יְהוָ֥ה צְבָאֽוֹת׃	
בְּרִיתִ֣י ׀ הָיְתָ֣ה אִתּ֗וֹ הַחַיִּים֙ וְהַשָּׁל֔וֹם ⁵	**5** II. Love for God's Word
וָאֶתְּנֵֽם־ל֥וֹ	
מוֹרָ֖א	
וַיִּֽירָאֵ֑נִי	
וּמִפְּנֵ֥י שְׁמִ֖י נִחַ֥ת הֽוּא׃	
תּוֹרַ֤ת אֱמֶת֙ הָיְתָ֣ה בְּפִ֔יהוּ ⁶	**6**
וְעַוְלָ֖ה לֹא־נִמְצָ֣א בִשְׂפָתָ֑יו	
בְּשָׁל֤וֹם	
וּבְמִישׁוֹר֙	
הָלַ֣ךְ אִתִּ֔י	
וְרַבִּ֖ים הֵשִׁ֥יב מֵעָוֺֽן׃	
כִּֽי־שִׂפְתֵ֤י כֹהֵן֙ יִשְׁמְרוּ־דַ֔עַת ⁷	**7**
וְתוֹרָ֖ה יְבַקְשׁ֣וּ מִפִּ֑יהוּ	
כִּ֛י מַלְאַ֥ךְ יְהוָֽה־צְבָא֖וֹת הֽוּא׃	
וְאַתֶּם֙ סַרְתֶּ֣ם מִן־הַדֶּ֔רֶךְ ⁸	**8**
הִכְשַׁלְתֶּ֥ם רַבִּ֖ים בַּתּוֹרָ֑ה	
שִֽׁחַתֶּם֙ בְּרִ֣ית הַלֵּוִ֔י	
אָמַ֖ר יְהוָ֥ה צְבָאֽוֹת׃	
וְגַם־אֲנִ֞י נָתַ֧תִּי אֶתְכֶ֛ם ⁹	**9**
נִבְזִ֥ים	
וּשְׁפָלִ֖ים	
לְכָל־הָעָ֑ם	
כְּפִ֗י אֲשֶׁ֤ר אֵֽינְכֶם֙ שֹׁמְרִ֣ים אֶת־דְּרָכַ֔י	
וְנֹשְׂאִ֥ים פָּנִ֖ים בַּתּוֹרָֽה׃ פ	

10   Don't we all have one father?

Has not one God created us all?

Why does each man act deceitfully to his brother

    thus violating the covenant of our fathers?

11   Judah has acted deceitfully

and has committed an abomination

    in Israel

and in Jerusalem

because Judah has defiled his holiness

    from the LORD

which he loves

and has married a daughter

    of a foreign god.

12   May the LORD cut off

from the tents of Jacob

the man who does this

    awaking

and answering

although he brings an offering

    to the LORD of hosts.

III. Love for
God's People

10

10 הֲלוֹא אָב אֶחָד לְכֻלָּנוּ
הֲלוֹא אֵל אֶחָד בְּרָאָנוּ
מַדּוּעַ נִבְגַּד אִישׁ בְּאָחִיו
לְחַלֵּל בְּרִית אֲבֹתֵינוּ :

11 בָּגְדָה יְהוּדָה
וְתוֹעֵבָה נֶעֶשְׂתָה
בְּיִשְׂרָאֵל
וּ בִירוּשָׁלִָם
כִּי ׀ חִלֵּל יְהוּדָה קֹדֶשׁ
יְהוָה
אֲשֶׁר אָהֵב
וּבָעַל בַּת־אֵל נֵכָר :

11

12 יַכְרֵת יְהוָה לָאִישׁ
אֲשֶׁר יַעֲשֶׂנָּה
עֵר
וְעֹנֶה
מֵאָהֳלֵי יַעֲקֹב
וּמַגִּישׁ מִנְחָה
לַיהוָה צְבָאוֹת :

12

13 | And you also do this:

Flood the altar of the LORD

with tears

weeping

and crying

yet he still does not { pay attention to the offering
or accept it

with favor

from your hands.

14 | But you say, "Why?"

Because the LORD was witness

between { you
and the wife of your youth

with whom you have acted unfaithfully

though { she has united with you
she is the wife of your covenant.

15 | Has he not made them one?

even though he had the remnant of the spirit?

And why one?

He is seeking a godly seed.

So you should be on guard for your life

and do not act unfaithfully with the wife of your youth.

16 | For { I hate divorce

says the LORD, the God of Israel

and wrongdoing has covered his garment

says the LORD of hosts.

So be on guard for your life

and do not act unfaithfully.

IV. Love for
God's Gift
of a
Marriage
Partner

13 וְזֹאת֙ שֵׁנִ֣ית תַּעֲשׂ֔וּ

כַּסּ֤וֹת דִּמְעָה֙ אֶת־מִזְבַּ֣ח יְהוָ֔ה

בְּכִ֖י

וַֽאֲנָקָ֑ה

מֵאֵ֣ין ע֗וֹד פְּנוֹת֙ אֶל־הַמִּנְחָ֔ה

וְלָקַ֥חַת

רָצ֖וֹן

מִיֶּדְכֶֽם׃

14 וַאֲמַרְתֶּ֖ם עַל־מָ֑ה

בֵּינְךָ֜

עַ֡ל כִּי־יְהוָה֩ הֵעִ֨יד

וּבֵ֣ין ׀ אֵ֣שֶׁת נְעוּרֶ֗יךָ

אֲשֶׁ֤ר אַתָּה֙ בָּגַ֣דְתָּה בָּ֔הּ

חֲבֶרְתְּךָ֖

וְהִ֥יא

וְאֵ֥שֶׁת בְּרִיתֶֽךָ׃

15 וְלֹא־אֶחָ֣ד עָשָׂ֗ה

וּשְׁאָ֥ר ר֙וּחַ֙ ל֔וֹ

וּמָה֙ הָֽאֶחָ֔ד

מְבַקֵּ֖שׁ זֶ֣רַע אֱלֹהִ֑ים

וְנִשְׁמַרְתֶּם֙ בְּר֣וּחֲכֶ֔ם

וּבְאֵ֥שֶׁת נְעוּרֶ֖יךָ אַל־יִבְגֹּֽד׃

16 כִּֽי־שָׂנֵ֣א שַׁלַּ֗ח

אָמַ֞ר יְהוָ֤ה אֱלֹהֵי֙ יִשְׂרָאֵ֔ל

וְכִסָּ֤ה חָמָס֙ עַל־לְבוּשׁ֔וֹ

אָמַ֖ר יְהוָ֣ה צְבָא֑וֹת

וְנִשְׁמַרְתֶּ֥ם בְּרוּחֲכֶ֖ם

וְלֹ֥א תִבְגֹּֽדוּ׃

17 | You have wearied the LORD with your words
　　　Yet you say
　　　　　How have we wearied him?
　　　　　　　in that you say
　　　　　　Everyone who does evil is good in the sight of the LORD
　　　　　　And he delights in them
　　　　　　Or, where is the God of justice?

1 | Behold, I will send my messenger
　　　and he will prepare the way before me
　　　even the LORD / . . . / will suddenly come to his temple
　　　/Whom you seek/
　　　even the messenger of the covenant
　　　　　in whom you delight
　　　behold he is coming
　　　　　says the LORD of hosts

2 | But who can endure the day of HIS coming?
　　And who can stand when he appears?

3 | for he is like a refiner's fire
　　and he is like a laundryman's soap
　　and he will sit { as a smelter / and purifier } of silver
　　and he will purify the sons of Levi
　　and refine them like gold and silver
　　so that they may present to the LORD offerings
　　　in righteousness

4 | ( ) then the offering { of Judah / and / Jerusalem } will be pleasant to the LORD
　　as in the days of old
　　and as in former years

5 | Then I will be near to you for judgment
　　and I will be a swift witness
　　against sorcerers
　　against adulterers
　　against those who swear falsely
　　against those oppressing { the wage earner of his wages / the widow / the orphan / the alien }
　　and who do not fear me
　　　says the LORD of Hosts

6 | For I the LORD do not change
　　therefore you, O sons of Jacob, are not consumed

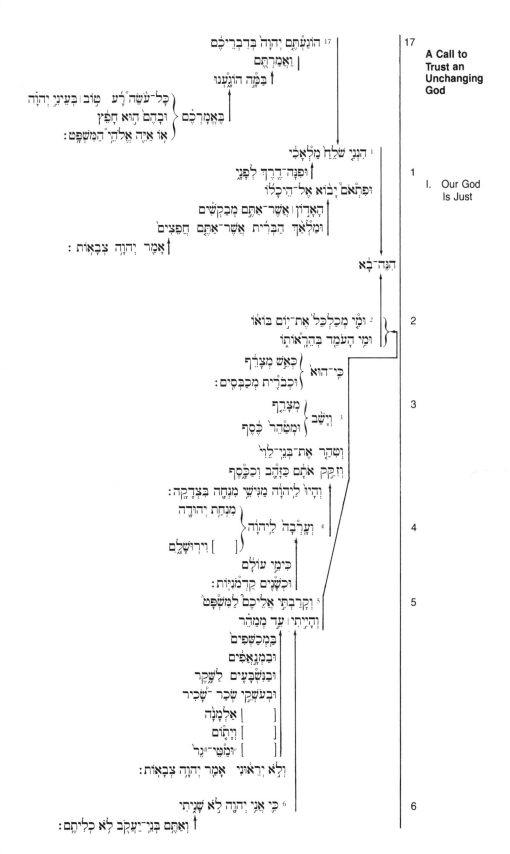

17 הוֹגַעְתֶּם יְהוָה֙ בְּדִבְרֵיכֶ֔ם

וַאֲמַרְתֶּ֕ם

בַּמֶּ֖ה הוֹגָעְנ֑וּ

כָּל־עֹ֨שֵׂה רָ֜ע ט֣וֹב ׀ בְּעֵינֵ֣י יְהוָ֗ה

בֶּאֱמָרְכֶ֗ם וּבָהֶם֙ ה֣וּא חָפֵ֔ץ

א֖וֹ אַיֵּ֥ה אֱלֹהֵ֥י הַמִּשְׁפָּֽט׃

1 הִנְנִ֤י שֹׁלֵחַ֙ מַלְאָכִ֔י

וּפִנָּה־דֶ֖רֶךְ לְפָנָ֑י

וּפִתְאֹם֩ יָב֨וֹא אֶל־הֵיכָל֜וֹ

הָאָד֣וֹן ׀ אֲשֶׁר־אַתֶּ֣ם מְבַקְשִׁ֗ים

וּמַלְאַ֨ךְ הַבְּרִ֜ית אֲשֶׁר־אַתֶּ֤ם חֲפֵצִים֙

אָמַ֖ר יְהוָ֥ה צְבָאֽוֹת׃

הִנֵּה־בָ֔א

I. Our God Is Just

2 וּמִ֤י מְכַלְכֵּל֙ אֶת־י֣וֹם בּוֹא֔וֹ

וּמִ֥י הָעֹמֵ֖ד בְּהֵרָֽאוֹת֑וֹ

כְּאֵ֣שׁ מְצָרֵ֔ף

כִּי־הוּא֙ וּכְבֹרִ֖ית מְכַבְּסִֽים׃

3 מְצָרֵ֤ף

וְיָשַׁ֨ב וּמְטַהֵר֙ כֶּ֔סֶף

וְטִהַ֣ר אֶת־בְּנֵֽי־לֵוִ֔י

וְזִקַּק֙ אֹתָ֔ם כַּזָּהָ֖ב וְכַכָּ֑סֶף

וְהָי֤וּ לַֽיהוָ֔ה מַגִּישֵׁ֥י מִנְחָ֖ה בִּצְדָקָֽה׃

מִנְחַ֥ת יְהוּדָ֖ה

4 וְעָֽרְבָה֙ לַֽיהוָ֔ה

וִירֽוּשָׁלָ֑͏ִם [ ]

כִּימֵ֣י עוֹלָ֔ם

וּכְשָׁנִ֖ים קַדְמֹנִיּֽוֹת׃

5 וְקָרַבְתִּ֣י אֲלֵיכֶם֮ לַמִּשְׁפָּט֒

וְהָיִ֣יתִי ׀ עֵ֣ד מְמַהֵ֗ר

בַּֽמְכַשְּׁפִים֙

וּבַֽמְנָ֣אֲפִ֔ים

וּבַנִּשְׁבָּעִ֖ים לַשָּׁ֑קֶר

וּבְעֹשְׁקֵ֣י שְׂכַר־שָׂכִ֗יר

[ ] אַלְמָנָ֤ה

[ ] וְיָתוֹם֙

[ ] וּמַטֵּי־גֵ֔ר

וְלֹ֥א יְרֵא֖וּנִי אָמַ֥ר יְהוָ֥ה צְבָאֽוֹת׃

6 כִּ֛י אֲנִ֥י יְהוָ֖ה לֹ֣א שָׁנִ֑יתִי

וְאַתֶּ֥ם בְּנֵֽי־יַעֲקֹ֖ב לֹ֥א כְלִיתֶֽם׃

7 | From the days of your fathers
You have turned aside from my statutes
and not kept them
Return to me
so that I may return to you
says the LORD of hosts
But you say
How shall we return
will a man rob God?
Yet you are robbing me
8 But you say
how have we robbed thee?
in { tithes
and
offerings
9 You are cursed
with a curse
for you are robbing me
The whole nation of you
10 (Bring the whole tithe into the storehouse
so that there may be food in my house
and test me now in this
says the LORD of hosts
If I will not open for you the windows of heaven
and ( ) pour out for you a blessing
until there is a lack of sufficiency
11 Then I will rebuke the devourer for you
so that it may not destroy the fruits of the ground
nor will your vine in the field cast its grapes
says the LORD of hosts
12 And all the nations will call you blessed
for you shall be a delightful land
says the LORD of hosts

7 | לְמִימֵי אֲבֹתֵיכֶם

סַרְתֶּם מֵחֻקַּי

וְלֹא שְׁמַרְתֶּם

שׁוּבוּ אֵלַי

וְאָשׁוּבָה אֲלֵיכֶם

אָמַר יְהוָה צְבָאוֹת

וַאֲמַרְתֶּם

בַּמֶּה נָשׁוּב :

8 | הֲיִקְבַּע אָדָם אֱלֹהִים

כִּי אַתֶּם קֹבְעִים אֹתִי

וַאֲמַרְתֶּם

בַּמֶּה קְבַעֲנוּךָ

הַמַּעֲשֵׂר

וְהַתְּרוּמָה :

9 | בַּמְּאֵרָה אַתֶּם נֵאָרִים

וְאֹתִי אַתֶּם קֹבְעִים

הַגּוֹי כֻּלּוֹ :

10 | הָבִיאוּ אֶת־כָּל־הַמַּעֲשֵׂר אֶל־בֵּית הָאוֹצָר

וִיהִי טֶרֶף בְּבֵיתִי

וּבְחָנוּנִי נָא בָּזֹאת

אָמַר יְהוָה צְבָאוֹת

אִם־לֹא אֶפְתַּח לָכֶם אֵת אֲרֻבּוֹת הַשָּׁמַיִם

וַהֲרִיקֹתִי לָכֶם בְּרָכָה

עַד־בְּלִי־דָי :

11 | וְגָעַרְתִּי לָכֶם בָּאֹכֵל

וְלֹא־יַשְׁחִת לָכֶם אֶת־פְּרִי הָאֲדָמָה

וְלֹא־תְשַׁכֵּל לָכֶם הַגֶּפֶן בַּשָּׂדֶה

אָמַר יְהוָה צְבָאוֹת :

12 | וְאִשְּׁרוּ אֶתְכֶם כָּל־הַגּוֹיִם

כִּי־תִהְיוּ אַתֶּם אֶרֶץ חֵפֶץ

אָמַר יְהוָה צְבָאוֹת :

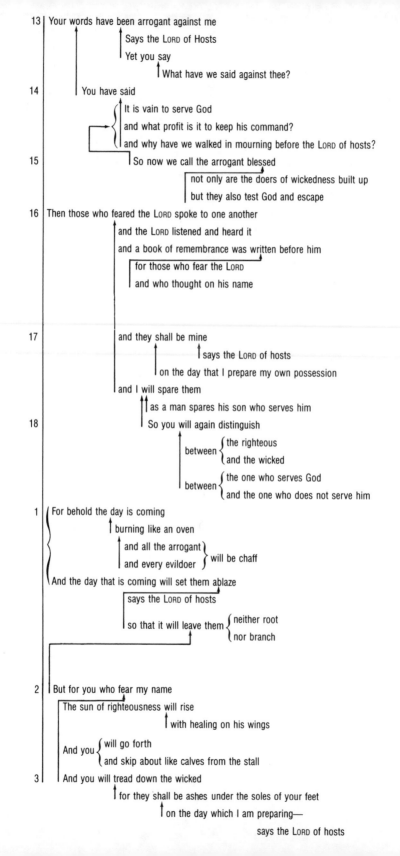

13 | Your words have been arrogant against me

Says the Lord of Hosts

Yet you say

What have we said against thee?

14 | You have said

{ It is vain to serve God

and what profit is it to keep his command?

and why have we walked in mourning before the Lord of hosts?

15 | So now we call the arrogant blessed

not only are the doers of wickedness built up

but they also test God and escape

16 | Then those who feared the Lord spoke to one another

and the Lord listened and heard it

and a book of remembrance was written before him

for those who fear the Lord

and who thought on his name

17 | and they shall be mine

says the Lord of hosts

on the day that I prepare my own possession

and I will spare them

as a man spares his son who serves him

18 | So you will again distinguish

between { the righteous
and the wicked

between { the one who serves God
and the one who does not serve him

1 | For behold the day is coming

burning like an oven

and all the arrogant }
and every evildoer } will be chaff

And the day that is coming will set them ablaze

says the Lord of hosts

so that it will leave them { neither root
nor branch

2 | But for you who fear my name

The sun of righteousness will rise

with healing on his wings

And you { will go forth
and skip about like calves from the stall

3 | And you will tread down the wicked

for they shall be ashes under the soles of your feet

on the day which I am preparing—

says the Lord of hosts

Hebrew	v.	
חָזְקוּ עָלַי דִּבְרֵיכֶם ¹³	13	**A Call to Take Inventory**
<div dir="rtl">אָמַר יְהוָה</div>		
<div dir="rtl">וַאֲמַרְתֶּם</div>		
<div dir="rtl">מַה־נִּדְבַּרְנוּ עָלֶיךָ :</div>		
אֲמַרְתֶּם ¹⁴	14	I. Is It Vain to Serve the LORD?
<div dir="rtl">שָׁוְא עֲבֹד אֱלֹהִים</div>		
<div dir="rtl">וּמַה־בֶּצַע כִּי שָׁמַרְנוּ מִשְׁמַרְתּוֹ</div>		
<div dir="rtl">וְכִי הָלַכְנוּ קְדֹרַנִּית מִפְּנֵי יְהוָה צְבָאוֹת :</div>		
וְעַתָּה אֲנַחְנוּ מְאַשְּׁרִים זֵדִים ¹⁵	15	
<div dir="rtl">גַּם־נִבְנוּ עֹשֵׂי רִשְׁעָה</div>		
<div dir="rtl">גַּם בָּחֲנוּ אֱלֹהִים וַיִּמָּלֵטוּ :</div>		
אָז נִדְבְּרוּ יִרְאֵי יְהוָה ¹⁶	16	
<div dir="rtl">אִישׁ אֶת־רֵעֵהוּ</div>		
<div dir="rtl">וַיַּקְשֵׁב</div>		
<div dir="rtl">יְהוָה</div>		
<div dir="rtl">וַיִּשְׁמָע</div>		
<div dir="rtl">וַיִּכָּתֵב סֵפֶר זִכָּרוֹן לְפָנָיו</div>		
<div dir="rtl">לְיִרְאֵי יְהוָה</div>		
<div dir="rtl">וּלְחֹשְׁבֵי שְׁמוֹ :</div>		
וְהָיוּ לִי ¹⁷	17	
<div dir="rtl">אָמַר יְהוָה צְבָאוֹת</div>		
<div dir="rtl">לַיּוֹם אֲשֶׁר אֲנִי עֹשֶׂה סְגֻלָּה</div>		
<div dir="rtl">וְחָמַלְתִּי עֲלֵיהֶם</div>		
<div dir="rtl">כַּאֲשֶׁר יַחְמֹל אִישׁ עַל־בְּנוֹ הָעֹבֵד אֹתוֹ :</div>		
וְשַׁבְתֶּם וּרְאִיתֶם ¹⁸	18	
<div dir="rtl">צַדִּיק</div>		
<div dir="rtl">בֵּין</div>		
<div dir="rtl">לְרָשָׁע</div>		
<div dir="rtl">עֹבֵד אֱלֹהִים</div>		
<div dir="rtl">בֵּין</div>		
<div dir="rtl">לַאֲשֶׁר לֹא עֲבָדוֹ :</div>		
כִּי־הִנֵּה הַיּוֹם בָּא ¹⁹	19 (4:1)	II. Is There No Difference?
<div dir="rtl">בֹּעֵר כַּתַּנּוּר</div>		
<div dir="rtl">כָּל־זֵדִים</div>		
<div dir="rtl">וְהָיוּ</div>		
<div dir="rtl">וְכָל־עֹשֵׂה רִשְׁעָה קַשׁ</div>		
<div dir="rtl">וְלִהַט אֹתָם</div>		
<div dir="rtl">הַיּוֹם הַבָּא</div>		
<div dir="rtl">אָמַר יְהוָה צְבָאוֹת</div>		
<div dir="rtl">אֲשֶׁר לֹא־יַעֲזֹב לָהֶם</div>		
<div dir="rtl">שֹׁרֶשׁ</div>		
<div dir="rtl">וְעָנָף :</div>		
וְזָרְחָה / ...... / שֶׁמֶשׁ צְדָקָה ²⁰	20 (4:2)	
<div dir="rtl">/לָכֶם יִרְאֵי שְׁמִי/</div>		
<div dir="rtl">וּמַרְפֵּא בִּכְנָפֶיהָ</div>		
<div dir="rtl">וִיצָאתֶם</div>		
<div dir="rtl">וּפִשְׁתֶּם</div>		
<div dir="rtl">כְּעֶגְלֵי מַרְבֵּק :</div>		
וְעַסּוֹתֶם רְשָׁעִים ²¹	21 (4:3)	
<div dir="rtl">כִּי־יִהְיוּ אֵפֶר תַּחַת כַּפּוֹת רַגְלֵיכֶם</div>		
<div dir="rtl">בַּיּוֹם אֲשֶׁר אֲנִי עֹשֶׂה</div>		
<div dir="rtl">אָמַר יְהוָה צְבָאוֹת :</div>		

4 | Remember the law of Moses

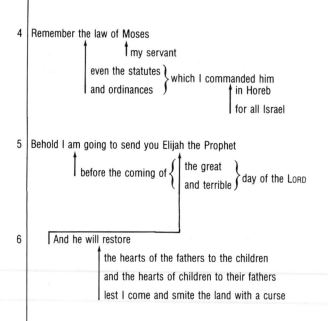

        my servant

even the statutes
and ordinances } which I commanded him

       in Horeb

       for all Israel

5 | Behold I am going to send you Elijah the Prophet

before the coming of { the great
and terrible } day of the LORD

6 | And he will restore

the hearts of the fathers to the children

and the hearts of children to their fathers

lest I come and smite the land with a curse

²² זִכְר֕וּ תּוֹרַ֖ת מֹשֶׁ֣ה עַבְדִּ֑י
אֲשֶׁר֩ צִוִּ֨יתִי אוֹת֤וֹ
בְחֹרֵב֙
עַל־כָּל־יִשְׂרָאֵ֔ל
חֻקִּ֖ים
וּמִשְׁפָּטִֽים׃

²³ הִנֵּ֤ה אָֽנֹכִי֙ שֹׁלֵ֣חַ לָכֶ֔ם
אֵ֚ת אֵלִיָּ֣ה הַנָּבִ֔יא
לִפְנֵ֗י בּ֚וֹא י֣וֹם יְהוָ֔ה
הַגָּד֖וֹל
וְהַנּוֹרָֽא׃

²⁴ וְהֵשִׁ֤יב
לֵב־אָבוֹת֙ עַל־בָּנִ֔ים
וְלֵ֥ב בָּנִ֖ים עַל־אֲבוֹתָ֑ם
פֶּן־אָב֕וֹא
וְהִכֵּיתִ֥י אֶת־הָאָ֖רֶץ חֵֽרֶם׃

Verbal Analysis (pages 4-5)

Author's meaning and the translations

Those who possess the skills of working with Greek, Hebrew, and Aramaic will want to translate orally the text in smooth-flowing but accurate English at this point. After the text has been translated and you understand all the words and their function in the sentences, you will want to compare the results with those of four or five English versions likely to be used by those who attend your class or church service. Even if you all use the same translation, it will be wise to compare your results with others.

If any significant differences appear, it is usually an indication that the text may have a special problem or contain an especially significant point just where the versions have differed. Do not bother copying the total translation of all of these versions or your own, but focus on those four or five rather significant or major differences and decide which translation best accords with the Biblical writer's meaning or single truth-intention. Record your reason alongside of your decision and use some format such as this one:

Example: Malachi 2:15a-b

RSV	"Has not the one God made and sustained for us the spirit of life? And what does he desire? Godly offspring."
RSV margin	"Has he not made one? And a remnant of spirit was his. And what does he desire? Godly offspring."
NASB	"But not one has done so who has a remnant of the Spirit. And what did that one do while he was seeking a godly offspring?"
NEB	"Did not the one God make her, both flesh and spirit? And what does the one God require but godly children?"
JB	"Did he not create a single being that has flesh and the breath of life? And what is this single being destined for? God-given offspring."
NAB	"Did he not make one being with flesh and spirit: and what does that one require but godly offspring?"
NIV	"Has not the LORD made them one? In flesh and spirit they

are his. And why one? Because he was seeking godly offspring."

My own   "Did not he [God] make them one?—even though he had the residue of the spirit [i.e., "enough creative power in reserve"] [presumably "to supply many partners"]. So why only one [partner]? Because he was seeking godly offspring." Reason: "One" is the object, not the subject, and the subject is God. The form of the first sentence is a question since an interrogative introduces the second sentence. The context is dealing with divorce, hence, the implication of marriage partners in the object "one."

Usually you will only want to record a single phrase or clause, and seldom will you meet a verse as difficult as Malachi 2:15 (it is one of the most notorious in the Old Testament because of its concise form and its implied subject and object).

Tropes and figures of speech

To be as aware of all figurative language as possible, consult E. W. Bullinger's *Figures of Speech Used in the Bible*.[11] In approximately 250 different figures of speech, Bullinger will list almost eight thousand examples—all helpfully indexed. See page 1066 for a discussion of sixteen of Malachi's fifty-five verses.

A list of the names of each of these figures of speech, along with their definition and the example found in Malachi, will greatly increase the sensitivity of the interpreter to these special nuances of meaning.

Theological Analysis (pages 6-7)

It is important to have a good handle on the words that are freighted with special or technical content due to their usage in the community of faith. These words may not always be spotted immediately by the beginner, but as one becomes more acquainted with the words and message of the Bible, a steady flow of earlier contexts come to mind as the interpreter studies the

11. E. W. Bullinger, *Figures of Speech Used in the Bible* (Grand Rapids: Baker Book House, 1968, [1898]).

selected passage. There are four ways we can get at these ideas. They include the use of: (1) key theological terms, (2) analogy of [antecedent] Scripture, (3) analogy of faith, and (4) commentaries.

Key theological terms

These terms may be garnered from: (1) general Bible knowledge, (2) chain reference Bible like Dickson Chain Reference or Thompson Chain Reference Bible, (3) topical Bible books like Nave's, (4) Biblical theology indexes and discussions, (5) theological word-books or dictionaries.[12]

Choose two or three of these words and develop a good word study on them. The basic source for word study is a lexicon and a concordance. This lexicographic study may be divided into four main divisions: (1) descriptive aspects (covering matters of form and function of the selected word), (2) distribution studies, (3) cognate or comparative aspects, and (4) contextual aspects.

Example: Malachi 3:16

"[They] thought on his name" [Hebrew, *ḥōšᵉbî*]

Descriptive study. The verb alone appears some 121 or 123 times in the basic *Qal* stem, the passive Niphal stem, the intensive/factitive stem of the Piel, and the reflexive Hithpael stem.

This verb is equally at home in the first four books of the Pentateuch, the books of the earlier prophets like Samuel, and especially in Psalms and Proverbs. But the prophet Isaiah—and to a lesser extent Jeremiah, Ezekiel, Micah, and Malachi—continue the use of this verb.

Distribution study. There appear to be six[13] clear variations of this basic root *ḥāšab* (meaning "to think," or "to plan"). The six may be schematized as in figure 4.

It is meaning "c" that we are concerned with. At this point, it would be well to isolate all contexts with this "infrequent mean-

12. See the bibliography and discussion of some of these tools in Kaiser, *Toward an Exegetical Theology*, pp. 131-47.

13. Leon J. Wood, "*Hāšab*," *TWOT*, 2 vols., ed. by R. Laird Harris, Gleason Archer, Jr., Bruce K. Waltke (Chicago: Moody Press, 1980), I. 329-30.

Figure 4
Meanings of *Ḥāšab*

Qal and Piel

(a) most frequent	(b) next frequent	(c) infrequent	(d) specialized	Only in (e) Qal	Only in (f) Piel
"planning," "devising," Zech. 7:10	"making a judgment," "to esteem," Isa. 53:4	running throughts through the mind, "meditating," "to think on," Mal. 3:16	"to impute," "to make a judgment," 2 Sam. 19:20	"to invent," Exod. 31:4	"account-ing" "book-keeping," Lev. 25:27

ing" and see what are the subjects, objects, and modifiers connected with it in order to sharpen the word picture and any special nuances we may gain from its *usage in context*. These last three words describe the heart of word studies. Studies based on supposed or real etymologies or root meanings are precarious at best since *usage* is the key to the meaning package.

Cognate or comparative studies. One may sometimes add examples of usage (and in consequence nuances in meaning) by consulting Semitic or Near Eastern cognate languages such as Phoenician, Ugaritic, Moabite, Akkadian, or Arabic. One may also consult the Greek word that the Septuagint translators selected, for often their words impacted the New Testament vocabulary. For example, Paul used this word in Philippians 4:8, "think on these things."

Contextual studies. If context determines the meaning of a word, then we must pay attention to the distinction between what is said and what is said *about* a word. Some lexicons (such as a Greek-English lexicon) print the first in italics and what is said *about* a word in roman type.

There are several contexts: (1) the verbal setting, (2) the historical and cultural setting in time, and (3) the theological setting. Each must be dealt with on its own terms if an in-depth definition is desired or if the word is a pivot word in the understanding of the whole pericope.

It must be borne in mind that not all words have an equal value or function. These are *idea words* (that have an inner content of their own, such as nouns and verbs), and *modifying* words (adjectives, adverbs,) and *relation words*, (which serve to link other words such as pronouns, prepositions, and some adverbs).

For all these reasons we conclude that "to think" or "meditate" on God's name meant to focus one's mind on that object so as to highly prize and attach great value to it. It was to be the believer's wealth, property, and most prized asset. It was a matter of taking a mental inventory and attaching great value to an object.

Analogy of (antecedent) Scripture

This is a matter of "inner exegesis," or a later Old Testament text quoting, alluding, or using key terms from an earlier Old Testament text in such a way as to continue the conversation and often to build on it.

In 1894 Robert B. Girdlestone[14] produced one of the few volumes that began to catalog some of these duplicate texts. But in addition to these direct citations, the Biblical books abound with ordinary formulae, short sentences consisting of watchwords, promises, and proverbial expressions as well as various allusions to earlier texts, persons, and events. Many older commentaries such as those of George Bush on Genesis through Judges supply these texts in the translation section of the book.

Until we have such a compilation in an "antecedent theology," convenient reference may be made to marginal references in most study Bibles.

Analogy of faith

For this category, one may refer to a systematic theology or a topical Bible like Nave's for the complete development of any Biblical term or theological concept.

It would also be well to list the New Testament texts that comment or quote on texts or ideas from Malachi.[15]

Matthew 3:1-12	Malachi 3:1
Matthew 11:1-14	Malachi 3:1
Matthew 14:2	Malachi 4:5

14. Robert B. Girdlestone, *Deuterographs: Duplicate Passages in the Old Testament* (Oxford: Clarendon Press, 1894).

15. I am indebted to E. W. Hengstenberg, *Christology of the Old Testament* (Edinburgh: T & T Clark, 1875), IV. 205-28 for this list.

Matthew 16:14	Malachi 4:5
Matthew 17:	Malachi 4:4-5
Matthew 12:12 and	
John 2:13-22	Malachi 3:1
Matthew 21:24	Malachi 4:7
Luke 1:16-17	Malachi 3:1; 4:5-6
John 1:6	Malachi 3:1
John 1:9	Malachi 3:1
John 1:15, 30	Malachi 3:1
John 1:27	Malachi 3:1
1 Cor. 16:22	Malachi 3:1; 4:6

Commentaries[16]

Now compare your results with others who have worked on this passage. Consult at least two or three of the best commentaries on your passage and make sure you are aware of all the issues they raise plus the evidence they handle.

Now *briefly* write up the results of your investigation of these commentaries by concentrating on the single strength or key points raised by these writers. But make sure you let these commentators talk to each other on any points of tension that surface between them. Be sure to enter the dialog yourself with key grammatical or evidential pieces of argument. Record all this very succinctly in not more than a page and a half.

Homiletical Analysis (page 8)

It is time to wrap up your study, and this is the most critical move you will make as far as the contemporary church is concerned. It will call for creativity, artistic skills, and faithfulness to the text in the process we have named "principlization."

Subject

This must embody either the climactic word, a memorable clause or phrase that epitomizes the pericopae, a text that functions as a fulcrum or pivot for the whole passage, or a

16. See Appendix B, "The Usefulness of Biblical Commentaries for Preaching and Bible Study."

repeated word that demonstrates the emphasis of the passage. But it must be deduced from the text, not imposed or foisted over the text as a grid.

Keyword

In order to keep the stance of the speaker and the listener unambiguous, it will be best to adopt as keyword an abstract plural noun such as "ways," "reasons," "concessions," or "lessons," so as to make all the main points of the lesson/sermon parallel and to view them from the same perspective.

That keyword should be suggested by the Biblical text itself. For example, if there are a series of clauses throughout the text beginning with "since" and which constitute its heart, then we may adopt a keyword like "concessions" or "consequences." If the text has a string of "because" clauses, then we may safely talk about "reasons."

Main points

Develop one of these main roman-numeral-points for each paragraph analyzed (the method for doing this is in *Toward an Exegetical Theology*, pp. 156-59). These main points should be constructed in parallel with each other and without references to any proper names except God. They should also usually contain first person plurals—us, we, or our, so that our listeners can begin applying in the very hearing and repeating of our outline.

Subpoints

Develop these as outlined in *Toward an Exegetical Theology* (pp. 159-60) with respect to judicious selection process and always with regard to the levels of indentation indicated in our syntactical diagram.

Conclusion

Now in one grand paragraph or two wrap the whole message or lesson up in a stirring summons, challenge, appeal, invitation, or indictment. What is it that God would have us to be, do, say, or think based on what you have taught in this passage?

Remember, we are ambassadors of heaven at this point, not our own representative. Therefore, we are not to beg our hearers or demean the gospel. We must prayerfully devote a good portion of our preparation time to thinking through just how we will phrase this conclusion and precisely what are the goals and challenges we will ask every obedient servant of Christ to accept. This is the final, but the hardest, test for every lesson: to note where the Biblical text led us and then imitate that goal in our own well-thought-out conclusion. Until God's Word has had a response from both the speaker and the listeners, all has been for nothing. It is simply a new idolatry; learning has become a "noun" instead of being a "verb" directed away from itself and requiring a response—in this case, to God.

Appendix B

The Usefulness of Biblical Commentaries for Preaching and Bible Study*

Karl Barth complained that recent commentators have not produced commentaries, "but merely the first step towards a commentary." Instead, he preferred the model that Calvin set in his commentaries: "How energetically Calvin, having first established what stands in the text, sets himself to rethink the whole material and to wrestle with it, til the walls which separate the sixteenth century from the first become transparent."[1]

Characteristics of a Good Commentary

What then is a good commentary? What are the characteristics of a useful commentary? After all, if the spiritual diet of a congregation may be fairly determined by an inspection of their minister's library, then the selection of Biblical commentaries, which normally make up the bulk of that library, will be extremely critical for the spiritual life and health of that congregation.

A commentary should exhibit the *plan, design,* and *scope* of the Biblical writer's thought. How can the interpreter understand any of the parts until the general pattern of thought and goal of the total book is known? It will be important to see how the arguments, logic, temporal sequence, or descriptions of the book

---

*Originally appeared in a slightly expanded form in *Christianity Today* as "What Commentaries Can (and Can't) Do" 25 (Oct. 2, 1981): 24-27.

1. Karl Barth, *The Epistle to the Romans,* (London: Oxford University Press, 1968), pp. 6-7.

hold together. Commentators must locate the seams between the various sections in a Biblical book and then show the unity, coherence, and relative degree of importance attached to each movement of the book from the perspective of the Biblical writer.

A second feature will be a clear outline of the train of thought in an entire book or epistle. When this is done effectively, it will clearly indicate all digressions, subordinate details, along with the main *train of thought* that contributes to the central aim of the book. This means that the connection of one part with another, the consistency, the ultimate bearing, and the various relationships within the book will be stated with crystal clarity and incisiveness—to the degree that they were developed by the Biblical author.

The third characteristic is most critical. Commentaries must now set about the task of setting forth the *meaning of the words*, phrases, and idioms of the original text. It is at this point that so many commentaries fail. Some are content to deal with what they are pleased to call the underlying history of the text and complete their comments and explanations with a statement (judged by many to be "scientific exegesis") about the literary sources from which this word in the text was taken or its sociological setting in life. Others, lauding the Scripture as the inexhaustible wisdom of God rarely settle for a single meaning of that text, but insist on finding various meanings for each word. Calvin, of course, did not deny the truth that this latter group of interpreters were praising, however he clearly affirmed: "I deny that its fertility consists in the various meanings which anyone may fasten to it at his pleasure. Let us know, then, that the one meaning of Scripture is the natural and simple one (*verum sensum scripturae, qui germanus est et simplex* . . .). Let us boldly set aside as deadly corruptions those pretended expositions which lead us away from the literal sense (*a literali sensu*)."[2]

A fourth feature will be a comparison of the teachings and sentiments found in one book with (1) those that preceded it in time (the analogy of antecedent Scripture) and (2) those that followed it in the progress of revelation (the analogy of faith). Only

2. John Calvin, *The Epistles of Paul the Apostle to the Galatians, Ephesians, Philippians and Colossians* (Edinburgh: T & T Clark, 1965), pp. 85-85; on Galatians 4:22.

within the last years has our generation rediscovered the significance and importance of theological exegesis. But this must not
become a ruse for sneaking in anything directly or remotely
related to the topics introduced in a book. This would only be to
concede that the subject-matter (*Sache*) was something beyond
the text—so far above it, that the text often becomes an imperfect
expression of it. In the hands of Karl Barth (and now sadly some
evangelicals), this means that "If Paul was struggling to express
the *Sache*, why should the interpreter be subject to Paul and not
rather join with him in this struggle, and say things that to the
interpreter were a better way than Paul's of expressing the
Sache?"[3] On the contrary, the written text as it was intended by
the Biblical author who first received that word as a revelation
from God must take first priority over any other consideration—
including subject matter and all analogies of Scripture or faith.
The commentator must, however, boldly point to any "informing
theology" which was antecedent in time to the present book being
explained and explicitly quoted, clearly alluded to, or used as the
theological platform on which the next stage of that same theological truth was being erected. This we shall call, for lack of a better
term, the analogy of (antecedent) Scripture. Only after the text has
been exegeted may commentators make similar connections with
the remaining corpus of Scripture (analogy of faith).

So keenly has the need for appreciating the theological aspect
of commentary work been felt that Brevard S. Childs wished to
reverse the whole process: "The fundamental error lies in the
starting point. It is commonly assumed that the responsible
exegete must start with the descriptive task and then establish a
bridge to the theological problem. . . . We are arguing that the
genuine theological task can be carried on successfully only when
it begins from within an explicit framework of faith."[4] Of course
Childs is right when he decries the alleged neutrality and
presumptuous historicism of many theologically bankrupt commentaries of the twentieth century, which prided themselves on

3. As persuasively argued by Daniel P. Fuller, *Easter Faith and History* (Grand Rapids:
Wm. B. Eerdmans Publishing Co., 1965), p.91.
4. Brevard S. Childs, "The Theological Responsibility of an Old Testament Commentary," *Interpretation* 18 (1964): 437-38.

their religious detachment. But is the answer to have the exegete interpret "the single text in light of the whole Old Testament witness, and vice versa . . . (letting) the circle of exegesis (move) from the specific to the general and back again?"[5] We think not. On this basis, every text in the Bible could potentially say everything and the same thing and, therefore, ultimately all would say nothing! No, let the commentaries make the theological connections—by all means—but let the order prescribed above guide that process. One method (analogy of [antecedent] Scripture) will aid the exegesis of the passage, and the other method (analogy of faith) will fill-out and trace subsequent developments of the same doctrine for comparing what is taught at one point in God's revelation with all that he went on to say. This latter information will normally be used in the teacher/preacher's *summary* of his sermonic points and not in his explanation.

Arguments Against Using Commentaries

Opinions about the usefulness and advantage of consulting commentaries varies widely. As Thomas H. Horne observed, "By some, who admire nothing but their own meditations, and who hold all human helps in contempt, commentaries are despised altogether, as tending to found our faith on the opinions of men rather than on the divine oracles: while others, on the contrary, trusting exclusively to the expositions of some favourite commentators, receive as infallible whatever views or opinions they may choose to deliver, as *their* expositions of the Bible."[6] The safest way is the middle path between these two extremes. But let us examine three different types of arguments set forth by those who reject all help offered by commentaries.

The first argument usually asserts that the Holy Spirit is the only one who can truly expound to our souls the real meaning of

5. Ibid., p.438. Against this list of four characteristics, one should consider the five criteria for selecting Old Testament commentaries raised by Terence E. Fretheim, "Old Testament Commentaries: Their Selection and Use," *Interpretation* 36 (1982):356-71. His list includes the commentaries' (1) scope, (2) format, (3) concern for theological dimensions, (4) underlying propositions, and (5) aspects of content.

6. T. H. Horne, *Introduction to the Critical Study and Knowledge of Holy Scriptures* (New York: Carter Bros., 1958), I: 353.

any text. Therefore, dependence on any man-made tools, such as hermeneutical rules or commentaries, is superfluous. Usually this argument is based on such texts as 1 Corinthians 2:14-16 ("The natural man receiveth not the things of the Spirit of God: for they are foolishness unto him: neither can he know them, because they are spiritually discerned") or 2 Corinthians 3:14-17 ("But their minds were blinded . . . even to this day; when Moses is read . . . [until they] turn to the Lord . . . [then] the veil shall be taken away . . . [for] where the Spirit of the Lord is, there is liberty").

However, neither of these two texts (or any others, for that matter) would make the ministry of the Holy Spirit an "open sesame" for interpretation. If that were so, why did the apostle Peter find certain things in Paul's writings "hard to understand" (2 Pet. 3:16)? The Greek word in 1 Corinthians 2:14 for "receive" has to do with the "welcoming" or "reception" of the teaching given. Paul is not arguing that there are two logics in this world, one pagan and one spiritual. Instead, he is saying that those who are devoid of the Holy Spirit have no realization of the worth, value, and personal application of the truths taught—that is the blind spot and the "veildom" pagans suffer. Meanwhile, they understand enough of what is taught to reject it as foolishness. We conclude that the Holy Spirit does not impart a meaning to the text which could not be gotten from the text itself, but he helps us overcome our sinful prejudices and pride so that we see that the text is addressing us in our particular sinfulness.[7]

A second argument claims that Scripture is already intelligible to those who possess faith; accordingly, all commentaries are unnecessary crutches.

The positive aspect of this argument is precisely the same point we raised for the ministry of the Holy Spirit. Certainly, when one approaches the text with a preunderstanding of faith, the text will be all the more "meaningful" (i.e., significant and personally relevant). However, faith cannot be an alternative avenue to knowledge and understanding, which operates outside of the ordinary functions of human understanding. When we speak of the clearness of Scripture to even the humblest and most un-

7. See Daniel P. Fuller, "Do We Need the Holy Spirit to Understand the Bible?" *Eternity* 10 (Jan. 1959): 22-23, 47.

learned of God's servants, we, with the Reformers, refer to the way of salvation. But sensible readers of the Bible will observe that "the Bible is also a *learned* book not only because it is written in the learned languages, but also because it contains allusions to various facts, circumstances, or customs of antiquity, which, to a common and unlettered reader, require explanation. . . . We may properly avail ourselves of the labours of inquirers who have preceded us; especially in clearing difficulties, answering objections, and reconciling passages which at first sight appear contradictory."[8] Faith then will be in evidence when the reader responds, acts, and personally applies what he has gained from a prior act of understanding of the text. In that prior act, the reader should not be embarrassed to judiciously use the assistance of carefully chosen commentators.

The last objection we will consider here is that commentaries are unnecessary since the Word of God has its own compelling power. Is it not "living," "active," "sharper than any two-edged sword" (Heb. 4:12-13)? Is it not the "power of God" for believers (1 Cor. 1:18) and as effective and certain in its mission as snow and rain are to the earth (Isa. 55:10-11)? Surely, it is like a hammer that breaks up hard resistance and like a fire which consumes (Jer. 1:9, 10; 5:14; 23:29). Where then is the need for exegesis, hermeneutics, or commentaries?

Scripture is powerful, not because of some supposed power that resides in words *per se;* instead, it is because these words were spoken with the authority of God.[9] Scripture is not invested with a quasi-magical force that in some mysterious or mechanical way short-circuits the need for helps offered in commentaries. Rather than the Spirit of God or the power of God imposing and forcing interpretations on the reader, both stand ready to assist in convincing, convicting, and aiding me to appropriate that word once it is understood. The reason the words of Scripture will stand forever is precisely because they are words from the mouth of the Lord (Isa. 40:6-8), and they are effective since they depend on the authority and the status of the one who utters them. The

8. Horne, *Introduction to Critical Study*, p. 353.

9. See Anthony C. Thiselton's brilliant essay, "The Supposed Power of Words in Biblical Writings," *Journal of Theological Studies* 25 (1974): 283-99.

suasiveness of the words, once again, resides not in a hermeneutical by-pass system, but in a power that is exercised in moral action and personal decision, viz, application or significance of the text; not understanding, meaning, or sense of a passage.

Not one of these three arguments is convincing. Instead, commentaries carefully chosen, should be like having experienced old friends along when one is traveling in a foreign country. Such a companion can point out what otherwise the unaccustomed eye might miss—especially if one is not acquainted with some of the objects and part of the road. Granted, "there are extremes; . . . it is no less wrong to place *implicit* confidence in the commentators than it is to treat them with contempt: to derive advantage from them, we should treat them as commentators *only*, and *not* as inspired writers."[10]

Defects of Existing Commentaries

There are five defects that appear in part or together in some commentaries which seriously damage their usefulness: four of these are listed in *The Encyclopedia of Biblical, Theological and Ecclesiastical Literature.*

The first is the prolixity or great size of some. When so much is said on so little text, then "it is almost superfluous to remark that such writers wander away without confining themselves to exposition. . . . It is very easy to write . . . anything, however remotely connected with a passage, or to note down the thoughts as they rise; but to *think out* the meaning of a place, . . . to apply severe and rigid examination to each sentence and paragraph of the original, is quite a different process."[11]

Another fault is to list various opinions or passages without sifting them. This type of commentary amounts to an anthology of previous commentaries on a text. But if no textual criteria are set forth for deciding between all this imposing list of names and opinions, what benefit is this new commentary? It has served only a secretarial function.

---

10. Horne, *Introduction to Critical Study*, I, p. 353 (emphasis his).
11. John McClintock and James Strong, "Commentary," *The Encyclopedia of Biblical, Theological, and Ecclesiastical Literature* (New York: Harper and Bros., 1868), II, pp. 428-29.

Other commentaries are notoriously evasive when it comes to tackling difficult passages. Plain passages are treated expansively, but when a perplexity arises the matter is avoided or glossed over. Alternatively, the commentary may lapse into an extended discussion on the difficult passage saying much *about* the problem but never penetrating the issue or suggesting the meaning the Biblical author had in mind.

A fourth and more common fault is that of superficiality. Usually this is the result of inadequate research and a failure to really live with the message of that book before the commentary was begun. Not all hens who cackle have actually laid eggs, and not all who write commentaries have made an original contribution to the history of commenting on that book.

In our day, the most serious defect can be found in a commmmentator's penchant for concluding his work after he has given a *descriptively* accurate commentary on the text while avoiding any responsibility for the problem of helping the church appreciate what may legitimately be derived as *normative* from that same text. The Reformers excelled in combining both of these features, and our generation must do the same if we are to be as effective as they were. That in part, was the point Brevard Childs was making in the article cited above. Robert M. Grant likewise felt part of this problem: "The minister needs some help in relating the part to the whole. An historical commentary is largely analytical. He needs some synthesis as well. Therefore, there must be commentaries of the patristic type, commentaries which relate individual passages and books to the whole of Christian theology and to the needs of the modern world. The minister must start with the message then, but he must come out with a message now."[12] I am not so sure that the formula for obtaining this help is as Grant suggested from Professor Cadbury:

$$\frac{\text{the author's message}}{\text{his environment}} = \frac{X}{\text{our environment}}$$

12. Robert M. Grant, "Commentaries," *Interpretation* 2 (1948): 400. Also note now Bernhard W. Anderson, "The Problem and Promise of Commentary," *Interpretation* 36 (1982): 341-55; and Fred B. Craddock "The Commentary in the Service of the Sermon," ibid.: 386-89.

Presumably, the problem of the commentator and minister is to locate X. But this is to reduce the issue merely to a contextualization problem. It is more persistent and deeper than that. It will depend on how effective commentaries are in relating syntactical and grammatical structures to their own message and then to the informing theology that preceded that text.[13] Only then am I ready to take the needs of my culture and day and apply the text to them in a legitimate form of principlizing.

Advantages and Proper Use of Commentaries

Thomas Horne gives some excellent advice on the use of commentaries. In the first place, a good commentary will be a model for our own interpretation. Cautions Horne, "We must not accumulate and read every interpreter or commentator *indiscriminately*, but [we] should select one or two, or a *few* at most of acknowledged character for learning and piety; and by frequent perusal of them, as well as studying their manner of expounding, [we] should endeavour to form (i.e., model) ourselves after them until we are completely masters of their method."[14]

The second use of commentaries is to help us understand what is obscure, difficult, or unknown in our culture or manner of speaking. In fact this is one method we can use in purchasing a new commentary. Quickly turn to a few of those passages in that Biblical book which are notoriously difficult and ascertain if anything original, penetrating, and methodologically fair is being done on those texts by this new commentary. In a very short time, you will be able to decide if this commentary is worth owning.

Even more important is the function of tracing the argument of a book so that one can at once set it in its wholeness as well as appreciate the way each section contributes to that unified plan. Many commentaries assume that the mere publication of their descriptively accurate topical outline fulfills this need, but it is worth little more than a schematic survey of some of the key topics found in that book. In this case, the genius of

13. Some of this procedure is illustrated in Kaiser, *Toward an Exegetical Theology*.
14. Horne, *Introduction to Critical Study, I*, pp. 353-54.

the book still remains beyond the reach of commentators and reader alike.

Finally, great commentaries will be of special help in aiding the interpreter set the theological and homiletical relevance of the meanings found in the passage. The scarcity or lack of exegetical integrity with which this one feature is carried out is enough to issue forth the call for an altogether new commentary in our generation, one that has among its key mandates the inclusion of this feature as part and parcel of its exegetical work. It will do no good weakly to attach it as an addendum or parallel idea from some noble, but less-gifted exegete. An exegete earns his right to enter into theological and homiletical applications of the text to the degree that the historical-grammatical-syntactical-cultural exegesis has been fairly carried out.

Perhaps no commentary will ever take the place of one's own study of Scripture. As Spurgeon challenged his students at Pastor's College and in his volume entitled *Commenting and Commentaries*, "A man to comment well should be able to *read the Bible in the original*. Every minister should aim at a tolerable proficiency both in the Hebrew and the Greek. These two languages will give him a library at a small expense, an inexhaustible thesaurus, a mine of spiritual wealth. Really, the effort of acquiring a language is not so prodigious that brethren of moderate abilities should so frequently shrink from the attempt.[15]

Neither should any interpreter be slavishly bound to judges, says Horne. Therefore, one should avoid reading exclusively commentators of one particular school. Often he will find valuable and important hints for elucidating difficult passages of Scripture even in those works which may be read with a certain sense of caution or even suspicion.

Above all, commentaries must be thoroughly honest with Scripture. As Spurgeon explained, too many preachers and commentators are like the Church of St. Zeno he visited in Verona where the ancient frescoes had been plastered over and obscured by other designs. "I fear," said Spurgeon, "many do this with Scripture, daubing the text with their own glosses, and laying on

---

15. Charles Haddon Spurgeon, *Commenting and Commentaries*, p. 47.

their own conceits."[16] Spurgeon went on to cite William Cowper's
lines from "The Progress of Error."

> A critic on the sacred text should be
> Candid and learn'd, dispassionate and free;
> Free from the wayward bias bigots feel,
> From fancy's influence and intemperate zeal;
> For of all arts sagacious dupes invent,
> To cheat themselves and gain the world's assent,
> The worst is—Scripture warped from its intent.

16. Ibid., p. 56

Bibliography

Commentaries on Malachi

Baldwin, Joyce. *Haggai, Zechariah and Malachi*. Downers Grove, Ill: Inter-Varsity Press, 1972.

Calvin, John. *The Twelve Minor Prophets*. V, Edinburgh: T & T Clark, 1849.

Feinberg, Charles. *The Minor Prophets*. Chicago: Moody Press, 1980.

Hengstenberg, E. W. "The Prophet Malachi," in *Christology of the Old Testament*, Vol. IV, pp. 139-228. Edinburgh: T & T Clark, 1875.

Keil, Carl Friedrich. *The Twelve Minor Prophets*, Vol. II, tr. James Martin. Grand Rapids: Wm. B. Eerdmans Publishing Co., 1954.

Laetsch, Theodore. *Bible Commentary: The Minor Prophets*. St. Louis: Concordia, 1956.

Mallone, George. *Furnace of Renewal: A Vision for the Church*. Downers Grove, Ill: Inter-Varsity Press, 1981.

Moore, T. V. *Haggai, Zechariah, and Malachi: A New Translation with Notes*. New York: Robert Carter & Bros., 1856.

Morgan, G. Campbell. *Malachi's Message for Today*. Grand Rapids: Baker Book House, 1972.

Orelli, Conrad von. *The Twelve Minor Prophets*. Minneapolis: Klock & Klock, reprint, 1977.

Packard, Joseph. *The Book of Malachi*, Lange's Commentary. New York: Scribner, Armstrong & Co., 1876.

Smith, John Merlin Powis. *A Critical and Exegetical Commentary on the Book of Malachi*, The International Critical Commentary. Edinburgh: T & T Clark, 1912.

Wolf, Herbert. *Haggai and Malachi: Rededication and Renewal*. Chicago: Moody Press, 1976.

Journal Articles

Althann, Robert. "Malachi 2:13-14 and UT 125:12-13." *Biblica* 58 (1977): 418-21.

Braun, Roddy. "Malachi: A Catechism for Times of Disappointment." *Currents in Theology and Mission* 4 (1977): 297-303.

Carmignac, J. "Vestiges d'un Péshèr de Malachie? [Malachie 1:14]." *Revue de Qumran* 4 (1963): 97-100.

DeLang, N. R. M. "Some New Fragments of Aquila on Malachi and Job [plates]?" *Vetus Testamentum* 30 (1980): 291-94.

Dumbrell, William J. "Malachi and the Ezra-Nehemiah Reforms." *Reformed Theological Review* 35 (1976): 42-52

Elliger, Karl. "Maleachi und die kirchliche Tradition." *Tradition und Situation: Studien zur alttestamentliche Prophetie.* Ed. Ernest Würthwein and Otto Kaiser. Göttingen: Vandenhoeck & Ruprecht, 1963: pp. 43-48.

Eybers, I. H. "Malachi - The Messenger of the Lord." *Theologica Evangelica* 3 (1970): 12-20.

Fischer, James A. "Notes on the Literary Form and Message of Malachi." *Catholic Biblical Quarterly* 34 (1972): 315-20.

Freedman, David B. "An Unnoted Support for a Variant in the MT of Mal. 3:5 [in Talmudic MSS]." *Journal of Biblical Literature* 98 (1979): 405-6.

Kaiser, Walter C., Jr. "The Promise of the Arrival of Elijah in Malachi and the Gospels." *Grace Theological Journal* 3 (1982): 221-33.

Kruse-Blickenberg, L. "The Book of Malachi According to Codex Syro-Hexaplaris Ambrosianus." *Studia Theologica* 21 (1967): 62-82.

Kuehner, Fred C. "Emphases in Malachi and Modern Thought." *The Law and the Prophets: Old Testament Studies Prepared in Honor of Oswald Thompson Allis.* Ed. John H. Skilton, Milton C. Fisher, and Leslie W. Sloat. Phillipsburg, N.J.: Presbyterian & Reformed Publishing Co., 1974, pp. 482-93.

Pfeiffer, E. "Die Disputationsworte im Buche Maleachi." *Evangelische Theologie* 19 (1959): 546-58.

Rehm, Martin. "Das Opfer der Völker nach Mal. 1:11." *Lex tua Veritas: Festschrift für Hubert Junkel zu Vollendung des siebzigsten Lebensjahres am 8 August 1961.* Ed. Heinrich Gross & Franz Musser. Trier: Paulinus Verlag, 1961, pp. 193-208.

Robinson, A. "God, the Refiner of Silver." *Catholic Biblical Quarterly* 11 (1949): 188-190.

Rudolph. W. "Zu Mal. 2:10-16." *Zeitschrift für die alttestamentliche Wissenschaft* 93 (1981): 85-90.

Schreiner, Stefan. "Mischehen—Ehebruch—Ehescheidung: Betrachtungen zu Mal. 2:10-16." *Zeitschrift für die alttestamentliche Wissenschaft* 91 (1979): 207-28.

Swetnam, J. "Malachi 1:11: An Interpretation." *Catholic Biblical Quarterly* 31 (1969): 200-209.

Torrey, C. "The Prophecy of 'Malachi'." *Journal of Biblical Literature* 17 (1898): 1-15.

Tosato, A. "Il Ripudio: Delitto e Pena (Mal. 2:10-16)." *Biblica* 59 (1978): 548-53.

Verhoef, Pieter Adriaan. "Some Notes on Malachi 1:11." *Nederduits Gereformeerde Teologiese Tydskrif* 21 (1980): 21-30.

Vriezen, Theodorus C. "How to Understand Malachi 1:11." *Grace upon Grace: Essays in Honor of Lester J. Kuyper.* Ed. James I. Cook, Grand Rapids: Wm. B. Eerdmans Publishing Co., 1975, pp. 128-36.

Waldman, N.M. "Some Notes on Malachi 3:6; 3:13; and Psalm 42:11." *Journal of Biblical Literature* 93 (1974): 543-49.

Wallis, Gerhard. "Wesen und Struktur der Botschaft Maleachis." *Das Ferne und nahe Wort: Festschrift Leonard Rost.* Ed. Fritz Maass, Berlin: A. Töpelmann, 1967, pp. 229-37.

Westermann, Claus. "Zuwendung und Wegbereitung (8 Dezember 1968) [Sermon Text Mal. 3:1-2, 23-24]." *Zuwendung und Gerechtigkeit: Heidelberg Predigten III.* Ed. Paul Philippi. Gottingen: Vandenhoek & Ruprecht, 1969, pp. 11-15.

Index of Scripture

Index of Names

Index of Subjects